Oh What Fun!

CHRISTMAS TRADITIONS

FOR KIDS FROM **1** TO **92**

by Suzanne Berry

GIFT BOOKS
from Hallmark

Acknowledgements

Special thanks to those who shared with us their stories, traditions, and ideas, especially those at Hallmark Cards and our friends at the Idea Exchange. Enormous gratitude to Trieste Van Wyngarden for her generous editorial contributions and heartfelt appreciation to Mary Gentry for her support and enthusiasm for this somewhat untraditional project. Lastly, deepest thanks to Theresa Trinder, whose vision was the impetus for this project, and whose research, creativity, and skillful direction ultimately made this the book that it is.

Published by Hallmark Books,
a division of Hallmark Cards, Inc.,
Kansas City, MO 64141
Visit us on the Web at www.Hallmark.com.

(page 27) "Year In Review" © 2005, National Public Radio, excerpted with permission.
(page 33) PEANUTS © United Feature Syndicate, Inc.
(page 59) Rudolph the Red-Nosed Reindeer © and ® The Rudolph Co., L.P.
All elements under license to Character Arts LLC. All rights reserved.
(page 62) It's a Wonderful Life © CinemaPhoto/Corbis.
(page 136) "Snow People" © 2005, The Washington Post, excerpted with permission.

Editor: Theresa Trinder
Art Director & Illustrator: Kevin Swanson
Cover Design & Concept: Mary Eakin
Designers: Brad Serum & Alison T. Bauer
Production Artist: Dan C. Horton

10 9 8 7 6 5 4 3 2 1

ISBN: 978-1-59530-161-1

BOK6073

Printed and bound in China

in memory of my grandparents
and their long tradition of love

Contents

Introduction

$\mathcal{P}$utting up the tree, playing your favorite Christmas album, baking cookies that make the whole house smell like a childhood memory . . . we each have our own way of welcoming this beloved time of year. The ways we celebrate, the memories we make, the traditions we carry on year after year—these are the things that make Christmas, well . . . Christmas.

Oh What Fun! is a celebration of those holiday traditions—the little time-honored rituals that make this wondrous season uniquely our own. Starting with the Christmas standards and a delightful look at how they came to be (you might be surprised!), this book explores how some traditions have been passed down through the ages and adapted by fun-loving families like yours and mine. You'll also find heartwarming stories about others' favorite family traditions and creative twists on old classics you can try on your own.

But a word of caution: nothing will take the fun out of this book more than thinking of it as a holiday to do list. Christmastime is already packed to the seams with parties, activities, planning, and preparations. I doubt you need any book implying you should somehow squeeze in more.

Instead, I suggest you take this time and use this book as inspiration to embrace the things that really mean the most to you and your family. Are you truly happy at the center of a hopping holiday party with all your friends and neighbors? Do you prefer quiet moments with close family to reflect and renew the spirit? Is Christmas a time for reaching out and reconnecting with a long-lost friend or two? Focus on what the season really means to you, and you'll find the traditions that reflect who you are. After all, that's what makes a tradition so meaningful—it's an expression of the people who practice it. A tradition can connect us to our past, help us celebrate the present and all it has to offer, and build memories for years to come. What could be more meaningful than that?

As you'll see, the way we celebrate Christmas has changed through the ages. But some things stay the same: goodwill, good friends, and good times with the ones we hold near and dear. I hope your holiday traditions bring you all of that . . . and more.

Counting the Days

We can hardly stand the wait . . . please, Christmas, don't be late.
—THE CHIPMUNKS

Even before the final traces of Thanksgiving turkey and green-bean casserole have disappeared from the back of your refrigerator, it's begun. The sights and sounds, the hustle and bustle, the holiday stressing and ultimate blessing of this most wonderful time of the year. Christmas.

Whether you're the super shopper who's got her sneakers and game on by 5 a.m. or the type who'd rather settle in for a long winter's nap, the first of December marks the beginning of a month packed with festivity. There are marshmallows for toasting, parties for hosting . . . anticipation's in the air!

But let's be honest. Sometimes the most wonderful time of the year is also the craziest. Traffic's jammed. Commercials are telling us what to buy. Stores and parking lots are teeming with testy shoppers. And people like you and me—who generally "have it together"—are getting that crazed look in our eyes, wondering how on earth we're going to get everything done.

This is the point at which I'd like to suggest we slow down, look around, and take some time to savor this favorite time of year for what it really is. The month of December is a time of preparation—in our homes and our hearts. It's a time for gathering with the people who mean the most to us and for remembering the real wonder of the season. Even when these wintry days are at their shortest and darkest, there is a lightness about them. It's as if something is reminding us that when everything else hibernates, dies off, or fades to gray, joy and hope are just around the corner.

Every night during December, I leave a candle glowing in my window. Somehow, shining out into the dark winterscape, that simple little light centers me. When everything else on my seasonal to do list is snowballing, one quiet little candle reminds me of what this season of waiting and preparing is all about. Life is always going to be busy. Darkness will have its turn. But at Christmas, I remember once more how important it is to save a place for goodness and light, a hope-filled place that believes in the promise of good things to come.

Advent

𝒜dvent comes from the Latin word *adventus*, meaning "arrival." It's the period beginning four weeks before December 25 and is the Christian season of preparation for Christ's birth. The weeks before Christmas present a different kind of challenge for each person. Whether you use this time to prepare spiritually, physically, or both, chances are you find, every year, that there just aren't enough hours in the day.

So sit back. Take a deep breath. Think about what Christmas means to you and your family. And let that be your inspiration for the entire month of December.

THE ADVENT CALENDAR

The Advent calendar is a tradition with simple origins—little chalk lines to tally the days before Christmas. The first printed calendar was made in Germany by a man named Gerhard Lang. His calendar was made of tiny colored pictures attached to a piece of cardboard. Later calendars had built-in doors revealing a small surprise, like a winter scene, Christmas wish, or Bible verse. Gerhard's idea was hatched from a favorite family tradition—the Advent calendar his mother had made, which she drew by hand and filled with Gerhard's favorite candy.

ADVENT IN ITALY

Here's where the manger display originated. On the first day of the *novena*, the nine days before and including Christmas Day, the family sets up its *presepio*, or nativity. Each morning (or evening) they gather at the scene to light candles and pray.

During the *novena*, children write Christmas letters to their parents—to wish them a happy holiday, promise they'll be good, and (of course) make out their Christmas lists. Parents read these letters aloud at dinner. Then (gasp!), they throw them in the fireplace. But it's okay! The kids chant to *La Befana*, the mythical Christmas witch, as their wishes fly up the chimney to be granted.

SANKTA LUCIA

In dark, snowy Sweden, pre-Christmas festivities begin on December 13 with the Festival of Sankta Lucia. St. Lucia is the patron saint of light, and that's what this holiday's all about. Early in the morning, a daughter dresses in white robes and a crown of candles (battery-operated, thank goodness!) and wakes the family one by one with breakfast in bed.

Each town elects its own "Lucia Queen" as well, who parades through the streets with her attendants, all dressed in white, and "star boys" wearing hats decorated with stars. They visit schools, hospitals, offices, and churches, bearing coffee and sweets.

Opening Doors

I love the idea of opening a new door every day. And an Advent calendar lets you do just that. It automatically sets aside a few moments every day for a little reflection, a little time away from the hustle and bustle. Here are a few fun spins on the old Advent calendar tradition.

MINI STOCKINGS

You can knit them, sew them from old sweaters or scraps, or buy them during an after-Christmas clearance. When you have 25, stuff them with a tiny treat (personalized pencils, mini books, stickers, barrettes, you name it). Your kids will love counting down to Christmas with a little treat to look forward to each day. Spread the giving around and have the kids choose 10 or so treats for you, too. They'll be just as anxious for the days you "open" one of the stockings they stuffed.

ACTIVITY BOX

Somehow, the days of December fly by faster than Santa's reindeer. And those great plans for family time together always seem to take second place to other, more "important" stuff. Try this: sit down as a family and write down twenty-five things you'd like to do together. Don't be too ambitious, either. "Making s'mores" and "dancing in your pajamas" are just the kind of things you're likely to have the time (and materials) for. Each day, pick a piece of paper from the box and do whatever it is, no matter how pressed for time you think you are.

DOING GOOD

A good deed is a great antidote to the December "gimmes," when the "I wants" and "have-to-haves" are stronger than ever. This one's just like the activity box, but instead of things to do, focus on things to do for the other people in your lives. Again, this isn't the time to make yourself crazy. But small, simple gestures like "donate old clothes" and "bring Christmas wreaths to the nursing home" will yield great rewards—for you and your little ones.

A BOOK A DAY

A bedtime story can work a very special kind of magic, especially during the cold nights of December, when wound-up kids need a little down time. There's lots of variation on this tradition. You can simply have your child choose one story to read each day or night during December. If you're ambitious, you can gather the books ahead of time and wrap each one like a special present. Place them all together in a box or basket and let your children choose one to open each day. If you'd like, you can choose particular themes, like Christmas, winter, or family. Whatever you choose, you'll be happy to see your kids get excited about reading, and you'll really treasure these quiet moments together.

You don't have to break the bank to build your family's library. Bookstore bargain bins, used bookstores (in town and online), library sales, and book swaps are all good sources for great kids' books.

De-stressing December

If just thinking about Christmas makes you anxious, let this be the year you start a new tradition. Prioritize. Make a list of the ten (or two) things you must do before Christmas arrives. Put your energy into enjoying those things to their fullest . . . and save the rest for next year. Or cut them from your to do list altogether.

TIME-SAVERS & LIFESAVERS

Wrap one or two gifts a day, so you don't have a mountain of boxes to climb come December 24. Make it a family activity by taking the time to talk about the person the gift is for. Will he or she like what you've picked? When was the last time you saw this person? What's your favorite thing about him or her?

Writer's block? Postpone Christmas cards until after the new year. This way you can include a snapshot of the kids on Christmas morning.

Ask for help. This one may seem obvious to you, but may not be so obvious to everyone else. Husbands and kids actually like to help, and if you allow them a little creativity, you can recreate Santa's workshop in your own home.

Shop early. It may be too late for this Christmas, but don't be afraid to start thinking about next Christmas as soon as the post-holiday sales start. You'll get some unbelievable deals, especially on seasonal stuff. And let's face it, the only person who really cares about where you got a gift and how much it cost is you.

Time is money. You can't clone yourself (yet). But you may be able to splurge on a few things that will save you time and preserve your sanity for Christmases to come. The pre-lit tree. Ergonomic tape dispenser. Electric cookie gun. You deserve it.

No one's perfect. Not even you. Invite some spills, stumbles, oops, and uh-ohs, and you'll feel a lot more at ease. Chances are, your friends and family will, too. So the roast comes out raw in the middle. Pick up a fried-chicken family meal. You'll have something to laugh about next year, when everything goes according to plan.

Let It Shine

The month of December is literally the darkest month of the year. It's not until the day after the winter solstice (December 21) that the world starts to see the light.

If you're feeling busy, pressured, stressed, or down during this time, remember to look on the bright side. Lighten up! Try candles, lanterns, luminarias. Experiment with color. According to psychologists, red light has an energizing effect. Blue is calming.

However you decide to do it, let your heart be light as well. Let some weight off your shoulders, enjoy the beauty of the season, and bask in the sunny company of your favorite people.

We set up the (empty) nativity set on the first day of December and scatter the figures about the house. Each day, my son moves them closer to the manger to replicate their long journey. With his help, we all experience the age-old Christmas story a little differently every year. (We've lost a couple of wise men this way, so I wouldn't suggest trying this with an heirloom nativity set!)

—Katie Forrester, Toronto, Canada

When we were growing up, my family gathered around the advent wreath every day in December, and if my siblings and I had been good, we got to put some straw in the nativity's manger. And if we'd been bad, we had to take some straw out! Sometime after church on Christmas Eve, we placed the Baby Jesus in the manger. And no matter how good (or bad!) we were, there always seemed to be enough straw to keep the Baby Jesus comfortable.

—Shane Lewinski,
St. Charles, MO

Real Traditions

To try to counter the "greedies" my oldest child tended to get around Christmastime, my husband and I started leaving little notes for her around the house—positive things like "Do something nice for someone today!" or "Have a great time with Grandma!" She became convinced they were from one of Santa's elves and was so thrilled to find them that we continued the tradition with our other kids, leaving a note a day somewhere they would find them. My husband's favorite part was thinking up elf names. Bubba the Elf quickly became a family favorite.

—Sue Langley, San Antonio, TX

Season's Greetings

Wild and sweet the words repeat . . . peace on earth, good will to men.
—HENRY WADSWORTH LONGFELLOW

Nothing can brighten a cold, wintry afternoon quite like a pile of holiday cards and letters, spilling out of the mailbox like sparkling rubies and emeralds among the manila of every day.

There in the treasure trove are photos of growing families and favorite smiles . . . handwritten notes that conjure up sentimental memories . . . and yes, even the annual update from that one person whose life is simply perfect and who likes to share every painstaking detail with two hundred of her closest friends.

Even if it's just once a year, taking some time out of our daily routine to connect and reflect seems like a pretty good thing to me. Sure, it can be daunting when you're the one staring down a fresh stack of cards to write, address, stamp, and send away. But I've found that once I begin writing that first note, I remember how much I enjoy it. It's a time to take stock of the year and what's made it memorable and to focus my thinking, card by card, on the people who matter most.

As the days and months of this "digital age" fly by, there's something so refreshingly real about the simple notes, stories, and well-wishes we exchange every year. They reconnect us to what's tangible and true in our lives. And they help us mark time—and celebrate it—along the way. Otherwise, we might very well just plod along running errands and paying bills and forget to look around every once in a while and notice who and what makes life so good.

I know to the naked eye, the holiday cards and letters we share are nothing more than ink on paper. But look with the heart and you might find they really are jewels—capturing and reflecting back the rays of light our lives—and those we've touched—truly are.

The Christmas Card

The sending of Christmas cards as we know it started in London in 1843. Before that, people exchanged handwritten holiday greetings—first in person, then by mail. By the Christmas of 1822, the Superintendent of Mails in Washington, D.C., needed to hire sixteen extra mailmen, just for Christmas mail. Soon after, he petitioned Congress to limit the mailing of Christmas cards. "I don't know what we'll do if it keeps on," he said.

Oh, it kept on. Today, more than two billion Christmas cards are exchanged by mail each year in the U.S. alone.

FIRST-FAMILY CHRISTMAS CARD

Dwight D. Eisenhower was the first to send the official White House Christmas card in 1953. His card went to American ambassadors, members of the Cabinet and Congress, foreign heads of state, and government officials. The presidential recipient list gets longer each year, from several thousand in 1960 to well over one million in 2007. (That's a lot longer than the average American family's list of twenty-eight.)

Merry Mailings

The U.S. Post Office has been printing special Christmas stamps since 1962. So it's not uncommon to receive cards with a little holiday flourish on the envelope. But some Christmas card enthusiasts take it one step further and mail their cards from a very special city . . . with a very special postmark. Check the list below for a city near you. If you can't make the trip, don't fret. Many of these post offices will postmark and mail envelopes for you if you stamp them and send them to the P.O. about a month or so before Christmas.

Antler, ND
Bethlehem, CT, GA, IN, KY, MD, NH, PA
Blessing, TX
Christmas, FL, MI
Christmas Valley, OR
Evergreen, AL, CO, LA, MT, NC, VA
Frost, MN, TX
Garland ME, NC, NE, PA, TX, UT
Holiday Island, AR
Holly, CO, MI

Jerusalem, AR
Joy, IL
Mistletoe, KY
Noel, MO
North Pole, AK, CO, NY
Rudolph, OH, WI
Santa Claus, GA, IN
Santa, ID
Snowflake, AZ
Wiseman, AR

Christmas Cards: Sharing the Wealth

Picture this. It's a week or so before Christmas, probably some time after the kids have gone to bed. You're sitting up with a stack of blank greetings, a ballpoint pen, a good case of writer's block, and a very long night ahead of you. Sound familiar? Maybe this is one of those traditions worth rethinking.

Why not make your Christmas communications a job for the whole family? It's true that many hands—even little ones with funny handwriting—make light work. And quite possibly, your Christmas cards or letters will be better than they ever were before.

❋ Have everyone in the family choose one wish for your friends and families. Write (or stamp, or type, or collage) these words on your cards; then have everyone sign them.

❋ Snap a photo of the family holding a handmade sign. "Happy Holidays" or "Merry Christmas from the Johnsons" are good choices. Attach to blank cards with photo corners—or have postcards printed by a photo service.

❋ Make a Christmas comic strip. Enlist the family's best artist to re-create the year's most memorable events. Give your comic a clever name, like "The Super-Smiths" or "Christmas Crusaders."

❋ Try an acrostic. Choose a word like "Christmas," "merry," or "Noel," and write a holiday wish beginning with each letter in the word.

❋ A Christmas quiz will keep family and friends on their toes. Write the major events of the past year in question format. (Whose softball team went undefeated this year? Which movie did Shelby watch seventy-five times? What was Henry Jr.'s first word?) Print the answers upside down at the bottom or on the back.

❋ Get all hands on deck. Kids will love this one. Cut out a Christmas tree shape from green construction paper and glue it to a blank card. Let the kids dip their fingers in different colored poster paints to create fingerprints of ornaments and lights. Or use a blue card and make fingerprints of snow.

Year in Review: Kid-Style

There are lots of benefits to making the kids editors in chief of the family newsletter. First, you're off the hook of having to write the news yourself. Second, it gives you some time to actually sit and talk with your kids about the previous year. You might be surprised to hear what they got out of it. Third, it can yield poignant, unexpected, or just plain funny results. Here are some examples from one of my favorite radio segments.

Jeff Horwich of Minnesota Public Radio wanted to ask some children what they would include if they had to write an end-of-the-year summary, so he visited the third grade at Adams Spanish Immersion School in St. Paul to ask the students about the highlights of their year. "What do you remember from this past year?" he asked. "What were the most important things?" Here are some of their responses.

"It was a really good year. I have a better class, better math book, and I like third grade better than second."

"Well, I just found out I met my long-lost brother. He's kind of taller than me."

"People don't call me 'little kid,' and
I feel like I stand up to boys more
and I understand stuff more."

"For my birthday party, we went to
Crosby Lake and we were going up to
this cabin, and I got sick because my
feet got so wet, and we got a lot of
bruises from falling down so much times."

"And I was climbing up a rock and I fell
down. My fingernail jammed into the
rock. It was fatter than my toe."

"It was mostly the greatest year of my
life because, well, I got to finally have
my own dog."

"I just met a dog! And, well, she ate
a needle, but she pooped it out."

Christmas Cards: Getting Crafty

OK, now that you've signed, sealed, and delivered all those messages, you can finally breathe a sigh of relief. You've got a whole year till you see another Christmas card, right? Wrong! Chances are, every day brings another flurry of season's greetings—from your best friends, your employer, even your dentist. What on earth could one family do with all those cards? Here are a few ideas.

SCRAPBOOKING SUPPLIES

Is it baby's first Christmas? First Christmas together? Just another wonderful holiday worth remembering? Use the art and words from Christmas cards to embellish photos and other mementos from this Christmas—or start collecting memorabilia from Christmases past.

GIFT TAGS

Cut the front of the card into a rectangle, oval, or shape of your choice. Use pinking shears if you'd like. Punch a hole, write the recipient's name, and violà! A beautiful gift tag that's good for the environment.

PAPER CHAIN

Here's a traditional decor idea that gives the tree or mantel a crafty, kid-friendly feel. Cut card fronts into four strips lengthwise. Then chain them together, stapling (or taping) the rings closed.

CHRISTMAS CONFETTI

With a regular or shaped paper punch, cut out enough pieces to sprinkle on tabletops, under the tree, or inside packages.

GREETINGS GARLAND

Cut out your favorite sentiments and messages from the outside or inside of the card. Glue them to a wide ribbon (or cut slits and weave together) to make a simple, sentimental wall hanging or garland.

Real Traditions

None of my immediate or extended family live in town, so I get a lot of Christmas cards. A tradition I've come to love is to wait to open all the cards until Christmas Day or the day after, when I can sit down in front of the fire with a cup of hot chocolate and open them all in one sitting. It takes a couple of hours, but it is such a treat to read them one after another, because it feels like I've just had a lovely visit with people who mean the most to me.

—Diane Norris, Overland Park, KS

My wife and I traveled to our parents' house every Christmas—until one Christmas when both our daughters had chicken pox. So I set up the video camera and had the girls make a "virtual Christmas card"—a live and in-person greeting (or as close as we could get) from them to their grandparents. It was such a hit we do it every year—and keep a copy for our "archives."

—Greg Cho, Washington, D.C.

Last year I got bored with the same old Christmas cards, so I rummaged through some old photo boxes and made my cards out of funny candid photographs of friends and family. Each of my brothers got a photo of us as kids ripping open presents on Christmas morning. And for my college friend Suzy—a snapshot of her secretly stuffing her face with cookies and a note saying "Santa knows when you've been naughty!" Using a photo marker, I signed and addressed the back of each photo like a postcard, stamped it, and stuck it in the mail.

—Megan Delaney, Charleston, SC

Oh Christmas Tree

I always wanted a tall, elegant tree like the ones at the mall or on television. The ones that inspired gasps of little-kid wonder with their towering, triangular perfection. My brother, on the other hand, scoured the lot for a tree that needed "work"— any excuse to saw off a few branches. In the end, though, we always came away with the same old kind of tree. It never really fit my childhood vision of Christmas grandeur, but as it turns out, it was just right for us: Short. Sensible. Friendly. Kind of like Mom.

When we got home, we put on some Christmas music and began the job of making the tree our own. My brother set up his model trains in a wide circle beneath the branches, just like Dad did when he was a boy. I hung the angel ornaments an elderly family friend gave me each Christmas. And

Mom got out the homespun ornaments her grandmother had made years before, handing them to us to hang while telling stories about "Grandma Great," a woman we couldn't recall by memory but knew by love.

By the end of the evening, the tree would be sparkling, the dog would be sneaking sips from the tree stand, my brother's trains would be circling in their rhythmic lullaby, and we would all take a few moments before bed to just sit quietly and bask in the warm wintry glow. And you know what? Every single year, it was magic. Somehow, a transformation had occurred—in our home and our hearts—and all from one squatty little evergreen, bedecked in humble trinkets and tinsel.

I guess we all bring something of ourselves to a Christmas tree. Amid the hustle and bustle and competing voices telling us what the season's about, a tree becomes the quiet little place where we make Christmas our own. We gather around. We remember. And somehow we know we're a part of something bigger, something that's lasting and true.

Famous Trees

ROCKEFELLER CENTER

This giant tree (usually a Norway spruce) must be at least 65 feet tall and 35 feet wide, though the manager of Rockefeller Center Gardens prefers it bigger. Forest spruces don't typically reach these proportions, so the Rockefeller Center tree is usually grown in someone's front or back yard.

At the end of the season, the tree is recycled. The largest piece of trunk is donated to the U.S. Equestrian team in New Jersey to use as an obstacle jump. And the Boy Scouts (lucky bunch) claim three tons of Christmas mulch.

MAIN STREET, U.S.A.

Disneyland is the only Disney park to still display a live tree—a tradition that began in 1956. In 2005, the tree was completely gilded to go with the golden theme of Disneyland's 50th anniversary. And on top? That's right: Mickey's famous ears.

HOLIDAY BLOCK PARTY

Where can you find a thirty-foot tree made of more than 245,000 tiny green bricks? If you guessed LEGOLAND,® you're right. This one's decorated with more than 240 ornaments and

100 candles, and greets visitors as they enter the park. Workers don't even think about taking down this tree until the weeklong festivities are over.

CHARLIE BROWN'S TREE

In 1965, this little tree captured the hearts of 15.4 million viewers. Lucy sends Charlie out to get the biggest aluminum tree he can find (a pink one, if possible), but Charlie returns with this scraggly little pine. "I ruin everything," Charlie laments, but soon discovers a little love is all it takes to transform the homely twig into a simple little symbol for what Christmas is all about.

Christmas Tree Firsts

Evergreen trees had mythical connections well before the first Christmas. Keeping their leaves and color all year, they've been a long-time symbol of life. No one is certain where the "first" Christmas tree came from, but it's a tradition that spans thousands of winter celebrations. Here are some highlights.

1000 B.C. Early Anglo-Saxons celebrate the winter solstice (the shortest day of the year) by decorating fir trees and burning the Yule log. The green of the tree and the warmth of the fire signal that spring is coming and life is good!

1500 One evening, as legend has it, Martin Luther took a walk through the forest. The sparkling of the stars through the branches made such a beautiful sight that he was inspired to bring a small evergreen indoors and decorate it with glowing candles—to show his children the "light of Christ."

200 B.C. The Romans celebrate a similar occasion, decorating their houses with greenery, exchanging branches with friends for luck, and parading decorated trees around town. It starts as a one-day event and quickly evolves into a week-long party.

1851 The first Christmas tree lot is set up on a New York City sidewalk. It sells out of inventory in several hours.

1959 The "Evergleam," the famous bright metal tree lit by a turning colored wheel, is born in Manitowoc, Wisconsin, the Aluminum Cookware Capital of the World.

1856 Franklin Pierce becomes the first American President to put up a Christmas tree in the White House. (Fifty years later, staunch conservationist Teddy Roosevelt bans this tradition, but his sons find a way to smuggle a tree into their bedroom.)

1999 The world's tallest-ever Christmas tree, a 276-foot eucalyptus, is lit in Tasmania's Styx Valley. It is host to more than 3000 solar-powered lights and a 13-foot star.

The Family Tree: Make It More Family-Friendly

CELEBRATING ROOTS

Buy inexpensive ornament frames in bulk during an after-Christmas clearance sale. (For a less formal look, make frames from jar lids, Popsicle sticks, or pipe cleaners.) Insert pictures of family members, going back as far as you can. Write names and birth dates on the ornaments, and you've got instant keepsakes. Allow kids to participate, and they'll really enjoy learning about their family tree.

TOKENS OF AFFECTION

Keep mementos from special occasions during the year: tickets from *The Nutcracker* or a football game, collectors' spoons or thimbles, seashells, anything that reminds you of a great time you spent together. Drill holes for hooks or tie ribbons around them to hang. Instant nostalgia!

MAKING YOUR MARK

Cut a tree skirt from washable felt, canvas, or other durable material and, each year, have your children "sign" it with a handprint, footprint, drawing, or short message. Use paint or permanent marker. If you're skilled with a needle and thread (or know someone who is), use a pen, then embroider over the lines.

GROUP EFFORT

Make choosing the tree a family decision. Before the search, allow everyone to choose the quality they're looking for. Start simple, with "green," "smells nice," or "higher than my knee." Bring the list with you to the lot and allow the kids to read and check off the items. They'll enjoy feeling like they're in charge.

CHRISTMAS WISHES

After the tree is set up, ask each family member to make a wish for Christmas. Write each wish on a small piece of paper, punch a hole, and hang the wishes on the tree through the holiday. When it's time to take the tree down, read and talk about the family's wishes. Did they come true? Store the wishes with your Christmas ornaments and put favorites up in following years.

Treecycling

You recycle cans, bottles, and newspapers . . . why not go green with your Christmas tree? More than thirty-three million real trees are sold in North America every year, which makes tree recycling a great way to give a little Christmas present back to the environment.

Visit **earth911.com** to find your local recycling center. You can also print out a paper ornament for your tree to remind you to recycle.

When my stepdaughter's daughter, Madalin, became enamored with an ornament on our Christmas tree, we let her take it home with her to Albuquerque. Each Christmas since then, we've encouraged Madalin to pick an ornament off the tree to keep as her own. Admiring and talking about the ornament she's chosen is a holiday moment I cherish and look forward to. We're looking forward to including our two stepgrandsons in this little holiday tradition when they are a year or two older.

—Pat Kelmel, Lee's Summit, MO

I was afraid my two-year-old would try to eat the ornaments— as my niece had done the year before. So I decorated the tree with strings of popcorn. For many years, all our tree decorations were edible. Now it has become custom for family and friends to come over and string popcorn for the tree while reminiscing about when our kids were small. (The kids like these stories just as much as we do.)

—Dalena Corcoran, Moscow, PA

I was always struck by the need my friends and neighbors felt to get the biggest, most expensive Christmas tree. So one year we started a tradition of going out on Christmas Eve and claiming the last tree in the lot. These trees always seem so sad at first, but when we finish decorating them, they're almost like part of the family, and more beautiful than we ever could have imagined.

—Kerstin Benoit, West Bloomfield, MI

Real Traditions

It's Beginning to Look a Lot Like Christmas

*Christmas waves a magic wand over this world,
and behold, everything is softer and more beautiful.*

—NORMAN VINCENT PEALE

Every year during Christmastime, I take a stroll through a glamorous local department store. Coming from humble small-town roots myself, the big-city feel of their elaborate displays still amazes and delights me. One year, the look was chic, wintry white. Next time, everything shimmered icicle-clean with elegant crystal. And lest we got a little bored, one bold year they'd dressed dozens of trees in coordinating shades of teal and hot pink. *Huh?*

Now if your household is one that can pull off a similar feat of haute Christmas couture, I certainly tip my last-season hat to you. But the decorations I know—the ones that come back year after year—are kind of a motley crew. I've got the hand-me-down twinkle lights. The down-to-earth angel who's seen better days. And the homemade Popsicle-stick projects no one clearly ever had the heart to throw away.

Presiding over this curious assortment, however, are a couple of prized pieces for which I have my grandmothers to thank. Above the fireplace hang Grandma Johnson's cozy red-and-green hand-knit stockings. And on the wall, a painting of a laughing St. Nick that Grandma Berry painted and displayed every December of my childhood.

Had I been schooled in fashionable department-store design, I would probably point to these as my fabulous *retro* pieces. In truth, however, they're simply the artifacts of years and Christmases gone by, tangible memories crafted by hands I've known well and deeply loved. Chances are, you have one or more of these treasures yourself.

But no matter your individual style—from fashionable to finger-painted—or whether you've got time to hot glue your household into holiday perfection, what I think all the decorating secrets in the world really boil down to is this: Decorate your home with love, however that looks to you. And you can be sure it will be beautiful.

Festive Favorites

Whether you're a decorating diva or not, you've probably had some experience with the following Christmas classics.

MISTLETOE

As if we needed an excuse to pucker up for a Christmastime kiss! Mistletoe's a longtime favorite tradition, but you may find its origins a little unsavory. In Old English, mistletoe means something like "dung on a twig," derived from the ancient (but not altogether incorrect) belief that mistletoe was propagated from bird droppings.

Nevertheless, mistletoe's been considered one of the most magical and mysterious plants— a symbol of life, love, and protection—and was hung from ceilings to ward off evil spirits. The kissing part came from ancient Anglo-Saxon marriage rites, as mistletoe was believed to have the power of bestowing fertility. And in Scandinavia, arguing couples would stand under the mistletoe to kiss and make up.

MISTLETOE 101: THE "RULES"

Everyone has their own rules for displaying the mistletoe and smooching underneath. Here are some of the traditional (if somewhat odd) rules and regulations.

* In some places, it's considered unlucky to bring mistletoe into the house before Christmas Eve.

* The first kiss should always be between people with different hair color.

* The first kiss under the mistletoe must not be between a man and wife.

* If you're not kissed under the mistletoe, you will not be married in the coming year.

* After each kiss under the mistletoe, you must pick a berry from the sprig. When all the berries are gone, the kissing's over.

TINSEL

According to an old German legend, tinsel was born when a poor woman did not have the means to decorate her family's Christmas tree. Through the branches, spiders spun intricate webs, which magically turned to silver on Christmas morning.

Actually, tinsel was made with real silver until the 1960s. It contained lead at one time, but today, of course, it's made of plastic.

POPCORN STRINGS

A uniquely American decoration, this one's provided hours of fun and busywork for kids of all ages. If you're a dedicated popcorn stringer, you probably have your own successful method. For those of you new to stringing corn, try the following tips.

❈ Don't use popcorn with any oils, flavorings, or butter. It's hard to work with and it can attract bugs.

❈ Let the popcorn sit for a few hours after popping. It'll be a little tougher and therefore easier to string.

❈ For variety, try stringing other materials in patterns. Cranberries and cereals are convenient, colorful choices.

NUTCRACKERS

Originally, nutcrackers were used to (surprise!) crack nuts. Eventually the nutcracker became a real art form, and especially beautiful ones were given as gifts to bring good luck and protect the home. Legend has it that a nutcracker serves like a guardian over your family, chasing away evildoers. (Hence the big teeth!)

Some say the nutcracker owes its popularity in the U.S. to American GIs stationed in Germany during World War II. Soldiers took a liking to the little guardsmen they found at German markets and returned home with them. And the popularity of Tchaikovsky's ballet, which reached America at about the same time, made nutcrackers the season's "it" toy.

Handmade Memories: Kids Can Do It!

*C*hristmas decorations are more than just knickknacks and doodads. Sometimes they're precious keepsakes handed down from generation to generation. And sometimes they're simply tiny handmade mementos made of macaroni or Styrofoam. Surely everyone has one or two such pieces of Christmas nostalgia. And if you don't, here are a few to try. A thing of beauty is a joy forever. Especially when you can say "I made it myself."

PINE POCKETS

These pretty, perfumed sachets—and the memories of making them—last a long time. And they're a great way to use up all those fallen pine needles.

Supplies: felt, fabric glue, pine needles, scissors, pinking shears, ricrac, buttons

Directions:
1. Double up felt and cut out shape (tree, ornament, heart, or star).
2. Run a fine line of glue about ¼ inch from edge all the way around one side. Leave a two-inch gap.
3. Glue sides together. Let dry.
4. Pour in pine needles.
5. Glue inside to close up hole.
6. Decorate with ricrac and buttons.

LITTLE ANGELS

Angels look sweet atop of the tree or lined up on the mantel . . . or just about anywhere!

Supplies: cardstock paper, feathers, pom-poms, pipe cleaners, glue, sequins, rhinestones

Directions:
1. Trace a semicircle on the paper (use a plate) and cut out.
2. Roll the paper to make a cone and glue (or staple) edges.
3. Glue on pom-pom for head.
4. With a pipe cleaner, make a small ring for halo and glue onto head.
5. Attach feathers for wings and decorate with sequins and rhinestones.

GLITTER GLOBES

What a wondrous thing a snow globe is! And it's relatively simple to make one at home.

Supplies: small jars with lids, small Christmas toys and figurines, waterproof glue, glitter, baby oil

Directions:
1. Wash and dry the jar.
2. Glue toys to inside of jar lid to create the "scene." Let dry.
3. Fill jar with baby oil, leaving one inch at top. Add glitter; let settle.
4. Apply glue to threads of lid, lower onto jar, and screw tightly. Let dry.
5. Give it a swirl.

More Merry

*A*re you someone who believes that "less is more" or is less always just a little bit, well, less? Whether you live on a sleepy little block or in a neighborhood you can see from space, you can probably appreciate the efforts some put forth at Christmastime to make their homes the happiest they can possibly be. Here's a story from *Hallmark Magazine* contributor Sarah Mueller about coming to terms with Christmas excess, electrically speaking.

CANDY CANE LANE

I grew up on a farm in Iowa, eleven miles from the nearest town. For Christmas, my mom insisted on a classy string of tiny white lights wrapped around our deck. It was frugal, understated, classy. I loved it.

Last year, my husband and I bought a little house in a quiet cul-de-sac. We were set to move in a week before Christmas—and drove by on Thanksgiving to take another look at our new neighborhood.

What happened? Giant, red-striped candy canes guarded the cul-de-sac's entrance, and our demure little house was all done up
in blinking lights, twinkling and flashing like a Vegas showgirl! We'd unknowingly bought a house on "Candy Cane Lane," a local street made infamous by its extraordinary showing of Christmas spirit—and decorations.

We still moved in. We bought some extra lights and threw them up in a few nervous hours. Then we hid behind the blinds and peeked out at the constant evening parade of minivans and SUVs. And that's when I started to get it.

There's a beauty in a silly surplus of holiday cheer. It's a beauty that gives up pretensions of respectability, of practicality. It's a beauty that revels in overstatement, in hyperbole, in twelve-foot inflatable lawn decorations. It's a beauty I'm beginning to embrace.

Sure, Christmas is about quiet reverence, but it's also about the kind of joy that can only be communicated through certain excess. After all, for every simple, awestruck shepherd, there's a wise man carrying extravagant baby presents across the desert.

Less Electric?

*D*ecided to go minimal this year? Power to you! Here are some ways to do less with lights and still feel festive.

❄ This one's an easy classic. If you have lights on the tree, position it in front of a prominent front window.

❄ Light the front path with luminaries and battery-operated candles. It's pretty—plus it's safe.

❄ Decorate just one tree in your yard with the lights of your choice. A lighted star on top is a really charming touch.

❄ Don't have a tree? Hang lights on something else you have at hand. A birdbath, antique bike, garden gnome. Be whimsical.

❄ Clip-on bubble lights are fun. Clip them to a wreath on the door for a funky twist on the traditional.

❄ Invest in the little plastic light clips made just for holding stringed lights. Install them once— and every year thereafter the job's half-done.

❄ Save effort and energy by following any of these tips and using energy-efficient lights. They'll use 30–90% less electricity (and you'll save 30–90% on the bill).

Let There Be Light!

Some say Christmas lights were invented in 1882, only three years after the invention of the lightbulb, when a coworker of Thomas Edison took some lightbulbs home to place carefully on the tree.

This made Edison's eyes twinkle with joy—and dollar signs. He starting making strings of lights just for the holidays. The trend spread to buildings in the early twentieth century when big-city department stores found that lit-up windows attracted more shoppers.

Light didn't appear on most homes until the 1940s, however, when they finally became affordable. Before then, one strand of lights cost $12. Today, that would be more than $150.

LIGHTS AROUND THE WORLD

An estimated 80 million homes are lit up for the holidays, and 150 million boxes of lights are bought each year. That's enough light to go all the way around the earth 28 times.

City Lights

From silver bells to lavish lights, cities and towns all around the world get dressed in holiday style at Christmastime.

In one diverse Oakland, California neighborhood, residents celebrate a sense of unity by cooperating with Christmas lights. They string lights from house to house, literally connecting every home and family on the street.

More than 100 people gather for Chicago's Magnificent Mile Lights Festival each year, where store windows display whimsical holiday scenes, carolers sing, and children get to view—and pet—real reindeer. The mile is, of course, lit up with more than one million lights. And as if that wasn't enough, after the lights are lit, there's a glorious fireworks display over the Chicago River.

"Nights of Lights" in St. Augustine, Florida, is inspired by the town's Spanish colonists, who placed a white candle in their windows to brighten the winter nights. Now, more than two million luminaries and tiny white lights adorn the palm trees, historic buildings, beaches, and lighthouses. There's also a torch-lit parade on foot and another parade of illuminated boats.

❅ Near Rovaniemi, just above the Arctic Circle in Finland, is Santa Claus' Village, a paradise of shops and sights like the Elves' Toy Factory and the Christmas House, where visitors can learn about the history of Santa Claus and Christmas trees. The village is decked out in traditional Christmas regalia, but if you just look upward, you'll see the aurora borealis—the finest, most magical display of lights there is.

❅ It's no surprise one of the prettiest displays is in Paris, the City of Lights. The Champs-Elysées was designed as a city park, but has since become a very busy, very fashionable avenue filled with shops, cafes, and theaters.

Let It Shine...and Shine...and Shine.

Everyone hates taking down the lights. If you're one of those people who just can't say goodbye to the holidays, use those little lights year round. They're great for illuminating a dimly-lit closet or pantry space, sparkling up the spokes of patio umbrellas, or scaring away monsters under a child's bed.

Growing up, part of my family's Christmas light-viewing tradition was to drive by all of the craziest yards—the ones that were so over the top with lights and puffy plastic characters. My sister and I would even take pictures. We totally loved it! Especially since our parents' decorating style was much more conservative. When my husband and I bought our first home last year, you can bet the first thing we did for Christmas was start our own lawn ornament collection. We started with three plastic Santas (you've got to ease the neighborhood into it, after all) but we plan to add to it every year. Someday we'll have the crazy yard everyone wants to drive by. It'll be a dream come true!

—Stephanie Young, Bloomington, IN

My family's from Hawaii. That means no cold weather, no snow, and no fireplace. But what would Christmas be without stuffed stockings hung beside the hearth? Thanks to my mom, I never knew. Each year, she magically transformed our traditional rectangular Chinese medicine chest into a fireplace with corrugated cardboard that's made to look like red bricks. We even had little construction-paper flames. On Christmas morning, my brother and sister and I woke up to stockings hung in a row and filled with goodies. It's our very stylish, very unique little family tradition, and Christmas just wouldn't be Christmas without it!

—Melissa Woo, Honolulu, Hawaii

Real Traditions

In 1945, Women's Home Companion *printed a knitting pattern for a Christmas stocking, which my grandmother made for my brother and me. When our younger brother was born, he got a stocking, too. As the family grew, my grandmother made more and more stockings—for our spouses and then our children (my grandmother's great-grandchildren!). When Grandmother could no longer manage the knitting needles, she passed the family Christmas pattern to me. (It was she who taught me to knit, after all.) And so I have carried on the tradition of making a stocking for each member of our growing family. This year I finished four stockings. Last year, I had a grandniece born on December 12, so I had to work furiously to get it done in time. I must admit that my stockings don't stretch as well as my grandmother's did—though my son has confessed to wetting and wearing his to stretch it to its full potential.*

—Sherri Millsap, Lawrence, KS

Stories of the Season

There are two Christmas stories my family and I simply cannot do without this time of year.

The first is the original—the story of Christ's birth in Bethlehem all those years ago. Every Christmas Eve as it's retold by candlelight, the same things about the story that filled me with awe as a kid still get me now: The singing angels. The mysterious star. The unlikely mingling of gift-bearing kings among shepherds and a stable of barnyard animals. I can't help but be amazed year after year at all the wondrous impossibility that came together that first Christmas night.

And the second story of long-standing family tradition? *National Lampoon's Christmas Vacation.* Okay, okay, I realize some people would probably consider it sacrilege to rate a goofball movie like *Christmas Vacation* anywhere near the story of Christ's birth. But it's true—it simply wouldn't be Christmas in the Berry family without the sidesplitting antics of Clark Griswold as he bumbles and stumbles his way through the holidays. Something about Clark and his well-meaning plans—and their bungled execution—just hits hilariously close to home.

As different as these two stories are in meaning, historical significance, tone, and oh . . . pretty much everything else, together they have a way of helping me make sense of what this holiday's about, exactly. On one hand, you have Christmas at its most inspiring and miraculous—the belief that hope and love greater than we could imagine can arrive in the most unlikely of places. And on the other hand, you've got Christmas as we actually experience it here and now, with our own real-life cast of characters. It's about our perfectly imperfect attempts to bring a little magic and wonder into our midst, whether with a grossly oversized tree or enough Christmas lights to shut down an entire city's power grid. (And to think those three kings found their way by the light of a single star.)

Whatever your favorite tales are this time of year, my only suggestion is to gather round to tell them, hear them, and savor the unifying moral of their story: Christmas is a time for both awestruck wonder and laugh-out-loud joy—a reminder that at any given time, something truly extraordinary can happen.

Story Time

The retelling of an old Christmas story is part of many families' favorite traditions. Here are some suggestions—a few old classics and a few newer tales—for great winter night read-alouds. (Fireplace, cocoa, and snuggly blanket optional.)

Cat in the Manger, by Michael Foreman

A Child's Christmas in Wales, by Dylan Thomas

"Christmas Day in the Morning," by Pearl S. Buck

Christmas in the Big Woods, by Laura Ingalls Wilder

"A Christmas Memory," by Truman Capote

"Christmas Trees," by Robert Frost

Circle of Wonder: A Native American Christmas Story, by N. Scott Nomaday

Federico and the Magi's Gift: A Latin American Christmas Story, by Beatriz Vidal

The Gingerbread Man, by Aim Aylesworth

"The Gift of the Magi," by O. Henry

How the Grinch Stole Christmas, by Dr. Seuss

Letters from Father Christmas, by J.R.R. Tolkien

The Mitten, by Jan Brett

"'Twas the Night Before Christmas," by Clement Clarke Moore

The Night Tree, by Eve Bunting

Olive the Other Reindeer, by J.otto Seibold and Vivian Walsh

The Polar Express, by Chris Van Allsburg

Santa Calls, by William Joyce

The Snowy Day, by Ezra Jack Keats

"The Story of the Other Wise Man," by Henry Van Dyke

A Wish for Wings That Work, by Berkeley Breathed

The First Christmas Story

Everyone knows a little something about the Christmas story—possibly the single most told and retold story in the world. Whether you remember the lines from studying them carefully yourself year after year or hearing them read by a pastor, parent, or even little Linus in *A Charlie Brown Christmas*, chances are, you remember them. And just in case you don't, here are a few.

And it came to pass in those days, that there went out a decree from Caesar Augustus that all the world should be taxed . . . And all went to be taxed, every one into his own city.

And Joseph also went up from Galilee, out of the city of Nazareth, into Judaea, unto the city of David, which is called Bethlehem . . . to be taxed with Mary his wife, being great with child.

And so it was, that, while they were there the days were accomplished that she should be delivered. And she brought forth her firstborn son, and wrapped him in swaddling clothes, and laid him in a manger; because there was no room for them in the inn.

And there were in the same country shepherds abiding in the field, keeping watch over their flock by night. And, lo, the angel of the Lord came upon them, and the glory of the Lord shone round about them: and they were afraid.

And the angel said unto them, "Fear not: for, behold, I bring you good tidings of great joy, which shall be to all people. For unto you is born this day in the city of David a Saviour, which is Christ the Lord. And this shall be a sign unto you; Ye shall find the babe wrapped in swaddling clothes, lying in a manger."

And suddenly there was with the angel a multitude of the heavenly host praising God, and saying, "Glory to God in the highest, and on earth peace, good will toward men."

From Luke 2, *The King James Version*

'Twas the Night Before Christmas

"Now, Dasher! Now, Dancer! Now, Prancer! Now, Vixen! On, Comet! On, Cupid! On, Donner and Blitzen!"

Most of us know these reindeer's names by heart. But before 1822, no one had heard of a single one of them. That's because they're the whimsical creation of Clement Clarke Moore, the man who most believe to be author of the most famous Christmas poem in history.

Can you guess what the author of this light-hearted little poem did for a living? Mr. Moore was a professor of ancient languages at a theological seminary in New York City. His most successful book (before this one, of course) was *A Compendious Lexicon of the Hebrew Language*. A tremendous work . . . but not nearly as popular with the kids.

Supposedly, Mr. Moore wrote his little Christmas ditty—which was actually titled "A Visit From Saint Nicholas"—during a family sleigh ride. (The driver reminded him of Santa Claus.) The children loved it, but Moore was so embarrassed by its "silliness" that he didn't even acknowledge himself as the writer until fifteen years after it was published.

But a little silly goes a long way! Since then, his little poem has seen thousands of different editions and translations. In fact, it is the most parodied poem in the English language. In 2006, an original handwritten copy sold for $280,000.

Rudolph the Red-Nosed Reindeer

You know Dasher and Dancer and Prancer and Vixen . . . but if you recall the most famous reindeer of all, it's probably because of the ever-famous animated television special that airs every year at Christmastime. The song was first recorded and made instantly famous in 1949 by singing cowboy Gene Autry. The animated special, which includes several other Christmas favorites such as "A Holly Jolly Christmas," and introduces us to all of Rudolph's misfit friends, has been a family TV tradition every year since it first aired in 1964. In fact, it's the longest running holiday special of all time.

The unique stop-motion animation style is referred to by producers Arthur Rankin and Jules Bass as "Animagic." Each doll, or puppet, was made of wired joints and operated inch by inch and filmed frame by frame to simulate fluid movement. Each individual scene required thousands of small, fine operations. In fact, the fifty-minute special took a year-and-a-half to film!

Technology has come a long way since 1964, though Rudolph and his friends have managed to delight and inspire kids of every generation.

Whether you're a reindeer with a shiny schnoz, an elf who'd rather fix teeth than toys, or a choo-choo with square wheels, chances are you know what it's like to be different . . . and how great it is to find a friend who likes you for who you are, no matter how neon your nose is.

A Christmas Carol

If there's one story that embodies the spirit of Christmas, it's Charles Dickens' *A Christmas Carol*. What other tale could have given us two such wonderful (yet opposing) forces of Christmas cheer (and gloom) as "God bless us, everyone!" and "Bah, humbug!" How many times in your life have you teasingly called someone a scrooge (or have been called a scrooge yourself)? Hopefully, not many, but everyone has their "Ebenezer" moments.

Dickens, frustrated with the ethics of industrial England, was working on a pamphlet called "An Appeal to the People of England, on Behalf of the Poor Man's Child." Lucky for us, he came up with an idea for a novel instead. He worked day and night on his "little scheme," and the book was written in seven weeks.

It was an instant success. In fact, the entire first edition sold out by Christmas. And amazingly, it's not been out of print since.

"I shall love it, as long as I live!" cried Scrooge, patting it with his hand. "I scarcely ever looked at it before. What an honest expression it has in its face! It's a wonderful knocker!— Here's the Turkey! Hallo! Whoop! How are you! Merry Christmas!"

"Why, it's impossible to carry that to Camden Town," said Scrooge. "You must have a cab."

The chuckle with which he said this, and the chuckle with which he paid for the Turkey, and the chuckle with which he paid for the cab, and the chuckle with which he recompensed the boy, were only to be exceeded by the chuckle with which he sat down breathless in his chair again, and chuckled till he cried.

From *A Christmas Carol*

SCROOGES THROUGH TIME

Not only is *A Christmas Carol* one of the most popular Christmas stories, it's also one of the most retold. From theatrical to television to cinematic stages, there's a version for every fan. Here are some of the most memorable.

A Christmas Carol, with Reginald Owen (1938)
Scrooge (A Christmas Carol),
   with Alastair Sim (1951)
Mr. Magoo's Christmas Carol (1962)
Scrooge, with Albert Finney (1970)
Mickey's Christmas Carol (1983)
A Christmas Carol, with George C. Scott (1984)
Scrooged (1988)
The Muppet Christmas Carol (1992)
A Christmas Carol, original Broadway
   musical (1995)
Blackadder's Christmas Carol (1998)
A Christmas Carol, with Patrick Stewart (1999)
A Christmas Carol: The Musical (2004)
A Sesame Street Christmas Carol (2006)

It's a Wonderful *Movie*

$\mathcal{I}$t's probably no surprise that on the American Film Institute's List of the 100 Most Inspiring Movies, *It's a Wonderful Life* ranks number one. It's the story of a regular Joe (or George, as the case may be) and his guardian angel, whose job it is to lift George's spirits just in time for Christmas. Whether you're a die-hard fan or a casual Christmas-Day observer, chances are, you've seen this movie more than once. I'd even bet you know a line or two by heart.

But here are a few things you may *not* know about Frank Capra's classic.

❊ The RKO Special Effects Department won a special award from the Motion Picture Academy for the film's fake snow—a mixture of foamite (a fire-fighting chemical), soap,

and water. Before that, they used painted cornflakes! But Jimmy Stewart wasn't happy with the noise they made hitting the ground.

❊ For the "Old Granville house" scene, Capra hired a markswoman to throw the rock at the second-story window. But Donna Reed insisted on doing the scene herself—and smashed the window on the first take.

❊ The set for Bedford Falls was one of the largest sets ever made for an American movie, covering four acres of RKO's Encino Ranch. It featured 75 stores and buildings, a factory district, a suburb, and a Main Street three city blocks long. And they built it all in two months.

❊ Many people believe George Bailey's hometown to be based on the real-life town of Seneca Falls, New York. Residents are so convinced of the similarities that they've renamed many streets after characters in the movie. There's even a Bailey's Ice Cream Shop—a real hotspot during the city's annual *It's a Wonderful Life* Festival.

❊ Two of Sesame's most famous residents, Bert and Ernie, share their names with Bedford Falls' police officer and cabdriver. Coincidence?

Christmas Movie Quiz

$\mathcal{E}$veryone's got a favorite Christmas movie. Some people even have two or three . . . or twenty! Test your cinematic smarts. Can you name the movies or specials these Christmasy quotes are from?

1. "We're your worst nightmare. Elves with attitude."

2. "Whew! Stay in here much longer and I'll really make a splash in the world."

3. "It's too early. I never eat December snowflakes. I always wait until January."

4. "We're all in this together. This is a full-blown, four-alarm holiday emergency here!"

5. "This is extremely important. Will you please tell Santa that instead of presents this year, I just want my family back."

6. "The best way to spread Christmas cheer is singing loud for all to hear."

7. "What a splendid idea! This 'Christmas' sounds fun. I fully endorse it—let's try it at once!"

8. "Faith is believing when common sense tells you not to. Don't you see?"

9. "Every time a bell rings, an angel gets its wings."

10. "It came without ribbons! It came without tags! It came without packages, boxes, or bags!"

11. "A toy is never truly happy until it is loved by a child."

12. "Just remember, the true spirit of Christmas lies in your heart."

13. "God bless us, every one."

14. "Well I double-DOG-dare ya!"

15. "Informed sources report that legions of junior citizens are making monumental efforts not to cry and not to pout. Meanwhile, letters by the thousands have been flooding postal facilities at the North Pole."

1. The Santa Clause (1994) 2. Frosty the Snowman (1969) 3. A Charlie Brown Christmas (1965) 4. National Lampoon's Christmas Vacation (1989) 5. Home Alone (1990) 6. Elf (2003) 7. The Nightmare Before Christmas (1993) 8. Miracle on 34th Street (1947) 9. It's a Wonderful Life (1946) 10. How the Grinch Stole Christmas (1966) 11. Rudolph the Red-Nosed Reindeer (1964) 12. The Polar Express (2004) 13. A Christmas Carol (1984) 14. A Christmas Story (1983) 15. Santa Claus Is Comin' to Town (1970)

Getting Personal

With all of the seasonal stories out there, you might be surprised to find that some of the very best are your own.

Want to tap into this wellspring of wonder? Try gathering the whole family (from kiddos to grandparents) and reviving the age-old art form of storytelling. Pick a time, such as Christmas Eve. Turn off the TV. Set the mood with a cozy fire or warm candlelight. Then take turns sharing the stories you love from Christmases past. Remember the blizzard that kept everyone snowed in until New Year's? Or that one time Uncle Joe set the tree on fire? The only thing bigger than the tales might be the laughs. Or tears. Or both!

From tales of how Christmas was celebrated way back when to stories about how Christmas changed when a certain child came along, everyone will learn a little something more about each other and what treasures the family history holds. And better yet, from one generation to the next, those memories will live on and on and on.

A good way to preserve holiday memories is to keep a Christmas journal. Make a note each year about the weather, special visitors, memorable gifts, etc. Take a family photo and add it to each year's entry. Then read from the journal every Christmas. You'll be amazed how vividly you all remember the year someone saw an elf peeking in the window or that long, long week when everyone was homebound with the flu.

Real Traditions

During Christmastime, my mother always read to my brother and me from a collection called The Tall Book of Christmas, which her mother had read to her as a child. We heard "Granny Glitten's Mittens" and "Giant Grummer's Christmas" so many times that I can practically recite them by heart! Though it was out of print for years, they re-released it last year, just in time for my son's first Christmas. I relished reading him the same stories that have been part of our Christmases for more than fifty years—and watching the little faces he made at all of my favorite parts.

—Melinda Gibson, Meriden, CT

Every Christmas Eve, my dad read "The Night Before Christmas." Being the jokester he is, he was always adding and changing lines to entertain us. (Like "I laughed when I saw him and spit on myself.") We came to love these hysterical moments and egged him on as we got older. When we moved away from home, we kept the tradition alive with a Christmas Eve "conference call." My dad comes to my house and reads to my kids, while my sisters' and brother's families listen along by phone in Indiana and Wyoming. And Dad's as hilarious as ever.

—Erica Paine, Palm Bay, FL

Every year, we're sure to watch A Charlie Brown Christmas when it's on TV. (It's not quite the same on DVD—there's something about knowing millions of other people are tuning in, too.) When he was younger, my brother always joined in the funky dancing scenes, and if we're lucky, we can convince him to do it now.

—Molly Klein, Detroit, MI

Yuletide Carols

Let heaven and nature sing!

If you love music, there's simply no better time of year than Christmas. Choirs are singing. Bells are ringing. Brass and string quartets are sounding joyful and triumphant. And everywhere you go, there's a seasonal soundtrack playing songs we know by heart.

Music is one of the oldest Christmas traditions there is, and it's one of my family's favorites. My grandmother, a retired music teacher, used to take full advantage of having her own personal "family band" to lead throughout the holidays. Everyone would literally gather around the piano as Grandma plunked out one jazzy carol after another and we sang along or played our respective instruments. Sure, we were always a little off-key. Our timing probably left something to be desired. And I'm sure the neighborhood dogs (had we actually been able to hear them) were howling at the ruckus. But the thing that mattered was that we were together, and it was Christmas. We were going to make a joyful noise.

Whether you sing in the community choir, host a neighborhood caroling party, or merely cheer on your favorite grade-schoolers in their holiday concert, be sure to allow yourself some time to revel in the sounds of the season. Because no matter our differences the rest of the year, for now . . . in this once-a-year moment . . . it feels like the whole world's humming the same song.

Come a-Caroling

*M*usic and singing has been part of Christmas celebrations for thousands of years. Caroling, or wassailing, is the tradition of traveling from house to house singing Christmas songs for the people inside. If you're lucky, your caroling tradition also includes eating, drinking, and socializing.

Wassailing began as an ancient agricultural ritual—a blessing of the apple trees. A group of wassailers would wind its way around the orchards, sprinkling cider or liquor on the dormant roots and singing *"Waes hael!"* (To your health!)

As the tradition evolved, carolers still sang, but carried the "wassail bowl," a big wooden vessel filled with mulled ale, roasted apples, eggs, and lots of other ingredients, from house to house to share good cheer. Soon, the carolers stopped carrying the wassail (possibly in Puritan communities where wassailing wasn't allowed) and began requesting refreshment from the people for whom they sang.

WHAT IS A CAROL, ANYWAY?

Originally, a "carol" was a traditional folk song people danced to. Later, the term included any song that was "festive." And since Christmas has long been the most festive time of the year, carols soon became associated exclusively with the holiday. Today, a carol is any song about Christmas in any way, shape, or form.

Behind the Music

"SILENT NIGHT"

It was a very silent night—literally—when this carol was written. The church organ was broken! Joseph Mohr, an Austrian priest, scribbled a poem and brought it to his organist and choirmaster, Franz Xavier Gruber, who finished the melody in time for midnight mass. There was music, thanks to Joseph and Franz, but it was played on the guitar.

"GOOD KING WENCESLAS"

The words were written in 1853, but the nearly 400-year-old melody may make this the oldest Christmas carol there is. King Wenceslas, patron saint of the Czech Republic, ruled Bohemia in the 10th century and was killed by his brother, Boleslaw. (A rather odd choice of subject matter for a Christmas carol, don't you think?) There's no mention of Christmas at all, but it does commemorate the "Feast of Stephen," which was celebrated on December 26.

"HARK! THE HERALD ANGELS SING"

Written by Charles Wesley, brother of Methodist Church founder John Wesley, this carol was originally written with slow, serious music. One hundred years later, Felix Mendelssohn composed a song to celebrate the invention of the printing press. Another musician combined Mendelssohn's music and Wesley's words to create the cheerful carol we know today.

"JINGLE BELLS"

Can you believe that "Jingle Bells," possibly the most famous Christmas song ever, was actually written for Thanksgiving? In November 1857, the composer wrote the song for the children in his Boston Sunday school class. It was so popular that it was repeated at Christmas that year and the next year and the year after that . . .

"WHITE CHRISTMAS"

"White Christmas" was written in 1942 by Irving Berlin and debuted in the movie *Holiday Inn* with Bing Crosby. The lyrics really struck a chord with World War II soldiers stationed overseas—and their families back home. It was such a hit that a later movie was made with the same name, which featured the song, of course, and an encore performance by Bing.

Sing-Along!

Since we learn them at a tender age and hear them year after year (sometimes hour after hour, depending which radio station you tune to), we sometimes commit Christmas songs to memory without even trying. Here's a list of 20 first lines from 20 popular carols. Can you sing what comes next?

Frosty the snowman was a jolly, happy soul . . .
Hark! the herald angels sing . . .
God rest ye merry gentlemen . . .
Rockin' around the Christmas tree . . .
I saw Mommy kissing Santa Claus . . .
Have a holly, jolly Christmas . . .
I'll be home for Christmas . . .
Jingle bell, jingle bell, jingle bell rock . . .
It's the most wonderful time of the year . . .
Oh, the weather outside is frightful . . .
Deck the halls with boughs of holly . . .
Said the night wind to the little lamb . . .
You better watch out, you better not cry . . .
Just hear those sleigh bells jingling . . .
Chestnuts roasting on an open fire . . .
Have yourself a merry little Christmas . . .
Here comes Santa Claus . . .
Up on the housetop, reindeer pause . . .
The first Noel the angels did say . . .

Heavenly Peas?

Sometimes, especially as kids, we bungle the words of even the most famous of carols. These invented lyrics are almost always harmless. And sometimes, they're very funny. Here are a few of the most common Christmas music "mishearings." Can you guess the songs they're from?

1. Later on we'll perspire as we sit by the fire.
2. No whale, no whale . . .
3. Oh how I love you, Frances.
4. The little Lord Jesus was eating the hay.
5. Fleas never die!
6. Oh come let us ignore Him.
7. Ho ho, the missing toe . . .
8. Sleep in heavenly peas.

Christmas Pop

Almost as long as there's been Christmas music, there's been pop Christmas music. You probably have your very own collection at home. Here's a list of some best-selling Christmas albums throughout the years. How many of them have you heard while rockin' around the Christmas tree?

Elvis Presley, *Elvis' Christmas Album*
John Denver & The Muppets, *A Christmas Together*
The Jackson 5, *The Jackson 5 Christmas Album*
Clay Aiken, *Merry Christmas with Love*
Nat King Cole, *The Christmas Song*
Raffi, *Raffi's Christmas Album*
Harry Connick Jr., *When My Heart Finds Christmas*
Dwight Yoakam, *Come on Christmas*
The Chipmunks, *Christmas with the Chipmunks*
Bing Crosby, *White Christmas*
Dolly Parton & Kenny Rogers, *Once Upon a Christmas*
Kenny G, *Miracles, The Holiday Album*
Ella Fitzgerald, *Ella Wishes you a Swinging Christmas*
Frank Sinatra, *The Sinatra Christmas Album*
Carpenters, *Christmas Portrait*
Dean Martin, *Christmas with Dino*
Garth Brooks, *Beyond the Season*
Andy Williams, *Merry Christmas*
Destiny's Child, *8 Days of Christmas*

Various Artists, *A Very Special Christmas*
Michael Bolton, *This Is the Time: The Christmas Album*
Jewel, *Joy: A Holiday Collection*
Amy Grant, *A Christmas Album*
Jimmy Buffett, *Christmas Island*
Bette Midler, *Cool Yule*
Louie Armstrong, *Christmas in New Orleans*
Johnny Mathis, *A 50th Anniversary Christmas Celebration*
Mariah Carey, *Merry Christmas*
The Wiggles, *Wiggly Wiggly Christmas*
Perry Como, *Greatest Christmas Songs*
Reba McEntire, *Merry Christmas to You*
Barbra Streisand, *Christmas Memories*
Christina Aguilera, *My Kind of Christmas*
Ray Charles, *The Spirit of Christmas*
Celine Dion, *These Are Special Times*
Mel Torme, *Christmas Songs*

Musical Events

BELLS OF BOSTON

Handbells, simple centuries-old instruments, come alive in Boston's historic Quincy Market. Over thirty choirs of bell-ringers participate in the Bells of Boston festival, and many continue to perform elsewhere in the city throughout the season.

CHRISTMAS SPECTACULAR

In 1933, the "spectacular" was simply a little show Radio City put on between film screenings. It wasn't until 1979 that the set was expanded to ninety minutes. Now, the show begins with a thrilling 3-D movie. And with over 140 performers, it attracts more than a million visitors per year. But two things haven't changed: The show has always featured the Rockettes. And it has always been a source of Christmas cheer in New York City.

A TUBA CHRISTMAS

The first TUBACHRISTMAS—a band of 300 tubas playing favorite Christmas songs—was conducted in New York City's Rockefeller Plaza Ice Rink in 1974. It was a tribute to the late tuba musician and teacher William J. Bell, born on Christmas Day, 1902. Now there are

TUBACHRISTMAS concerts every year in communities all over the world, where tubists of all ages come together to perform.

VIENNA BOYS CHOIR

The choir was officially founded in 1924 but is the descendant of the boys' choirs of the Viennese Court, which date back to the Middle Ages. Famous for their Christmas concerts, the boys perform about 300 concerts each year for more than half a million people, making them the most talented—and well-behaved—group of preteen boys on the planet.

ANGELS OF HARLEM

This is the endearing nickname for the touring members of the world-renowned Harlem Gospel Choir. Founded in 1986 by Allen Bailey, the choir is built on the teachings of Dr. Martin Luther King, Jr., and is comprised of the finest singers and musicians from Harlem's churches. The choir travels the world, sharing its joy and faith through music and raising donations for children's charities. The Christmas concert (last year at the Vatican) is an enlightening experience. You can see them every Sunday at B.B. King's Blues Club in New York.

THE NUTCRACKER

The story *The Nutcracker and the Mouse King,* by E.T.A. Hoffman, and the music by Peter Ilyich Tchaikovsky gave life to the legendary Nutcracker Ballet. The first show took place at Russia's Mariinsky Theatre, home of the Kirov Ballet. The Nutcracker appeared in Western Europe in the 1930s and in America a few years later. The dreamy, magical ballet has since become an annual Christmas tradition, showing in almost every city, and appropriate for all children, big and small.

GO SEE LIVE MUSIC!

You don't have to take our word for it. There's oodles of holiday musical events just waiting to be enjoyed. Check your local paper to see what's going on in your neck of the woods.

Making Christmas More Musical

$\mathcal{W}$e all love Christmas music, but sometimes the only time we really hear it is driving to and from work, or worse: the same couple of tired songs looped over and over in the department store. Here are a few ways to make Christmas music a more enjoyable aspect of this most musical of seasons.

DOWNLOAD, UPBEAT

Make a family soundtrack. Go to iTunes or Napster and choose twenty or so songs as a family. Allow everyone a couple of choices, and they'll be excited to listen to the whole CD, even your favorites, knowing they had a role as coproducer.

LET THE KIDS CHOOSE

Take the kids shopping and allow them to buy a CD of their own choosing. Where you might be tempted to go with the same old standards, they may be drawn to something different and fresh.

SUPPER SERENADES

Play music softly during family dinner time. Try to choose a different artist or style each night. Let whoever is on dish duty choose the evening's music. You may even get a few volunteers.

CAROL-SHY?

Too timid to go a-caroling? Or is it simply too cold out? Prepare a song as a family and perform it for a special person. Grandparents will adore it. Are they far away? Send a "carolgram" by phone or webcam.

EXPAND YOUR REPERTOIRE

This year, make it a point to learn a Christmas song you don't know. Try something older, with history, or if you know lots of those, learn the latest boy band's Christmas hit. Your kids will be shocked when they hear you singing it in the shower.

My holidays have always had a soundtrack: Elvis' Christmas Album. Year after childhood year, "the King" sang carols while my sister and I danced by the record player. (The slips under our velvety dresses made great tutus!) If we bounced around too much, Elvis would sing "In the Lane, In the Lane . . ." over and over until Dad came to fix it so the King could continue. On "Jingle Bell Rock," we skated across the linoleum in our tights, trying not to crash into the dinner table. I'm grown now, and that album is unplayable—scratched like crazy from decades of use. But a few years ago, after telling my sweet husband about this sweet memory, I found the Elvis Christmas CD in my stocking. The best part of all? It was recorded from the original album, so every song has that glorious record crackle that I've come to cherish.

—Amy Trowbridge-Yates, Kansas City, MO

Carrying on a tradition my wife had growing up, our family hosts an annual caroling party for other families with kids. Everyone arrives late in the afternoon, and the kids play or do Christmas craft projects while the adults enjoy some time to visit. After a bite to eat and brief rehearsal, we pile onto a rented bus (last year we had forty people!) and drive around to visit older folks who oftentimes aren't able to get out. Everyone's singing and the kids are keeping time with jingle bells and tambourines. Talk about a joyful noise! Our "audience" always seems glad we came, and sometimes we even draw a crowd. Then it's back to our house for hot cocoa and cookies. It's great having a party both parents and kids look forward to, and it's nice knowing how much it means to the people we serenade.

—Mark Mills, Phoenix, AZ

Real Traditions

Music at Christmastime was, and is, huge for my family. Every Sunday during Advent, my mother would light the Advent wreath candles at Sunday dinner and we would sing her favorite: "O Come, O Come, Emmanuel." Then, on Christmas Eve, it was the Eugene Ormandy Orchestra . . . on the original vinyl, of course. And Johnny Mathis! My mother was a big fan of his. So, at—and not before—the first snowfall of the year (the first sign that Christmas was coming), my brother and I got out the Johnny Mathis Christmas album and listened to it to our hearts' content.

—Maureen Gowen, Minneapolis, MN

Greatest Gifts

What if Christmas, he thought, doesn't come from a store?
What if Christmas, perhaps, means a little bit more?

—THE GRINCH

Anyone who experiences a Christmas morning with my family is always a little startled by our bizarre behavior. There are rude awakenings at the crack of dawn. Stealthy maneuvers to hide behind furniture. Secret notes stuck to coffeepots . . .

You see, one of the oldest traditions in my family is to be the first person to shout "Christmas gift!" to everyone you meet or talk to on Christmas Day. If you say it first, you're entitled to a gift from the other person. Hence the importance of catching your victim—I mean brother—by surprise.

Honestly, though (and I mean this), it's not about the gifts. I can't even remember a time that we actually got a present for being the quickest on the draw. "Christmas gift" is about starting the day with fun—and a little mischief. It's about putting a new twist each year on an old tradition handed down through generations. And maybe it's also a little about some longstanding sibling rivalry. But mostly it's about the tradition.

There's so much emphasis this time of year on the material gifts we give and receive. Everywhere you turn, there's hype around the season's "gotta-have" presents and pressure to live up to perceived expectations. No wonder it's easy to get caught up in gift-after-gift-after-gift giving and lose sight of the true spirit behind it.

When your shopping list starts costing you both your savings and your sanity, keep in mind that as great as it is to delight friends and loved ones with that perfectly picked present, in the end, the things we remember as our "greatest gifts" are surprisingly simple: The memories we make. The kindness we show. The little rituals of love and friendship we keep year after year. The rest? Well, that's just icing on the sugar cookie.

By the way . . . you there . . . the one reading this right now . . . one last thing before you go.

Christmas gift!

The First Givers

The three wise men (aka the three kings, aka the magi), an essential part of the nativity scene, first appear in the Bible in Matthew 2:1. The Bible doesn't say how many there were, what their names were, or how they got there. All that is filled in through history and legend.

It is believed that the wise men followed the star of Bethlehem, which led them to Joseph, Mary, and Jesus. And, according to medieval myth, their names were Melchior, King of Arabia (bringing gold); Gaspar, King of Tarsus (bringing myrrh); and Balthasar, King of Ethiopia (bringing frankincense).

Many believe that these gifts brought to the Christ child by the wise men may well have been the origin of our present-day custom of Christmas gift giving.

The First Gifts

And you think *you* get odd gifts at Christmas! Could you imagine trying to return frankincense to the department store? Actually, the gifts the wise men bore were very generous— and quite meaningful in their time.

GOLD

Who wouldn't want gold for Christmas? It's rare, and therefore very valuable. It's pliable, yet strong. It's the thing wedding rings are made of. It's also a symbol of royalty, which made it an especially suitable gift for the little King.

FRANKINCENSE

This is the fragrant sap from a tree that grows in Arabia and the East Indies. It was used in ancient times as medicine, perfume, and as a sweet-smelling incense during religious rites. It was also quite rare—and therefore quite expensive.

MYRRH

A valuable perfumed resin also from the bark of a tree. Because of its sour taste, it's named for the Hebrew word for "bitterness." It was used mainly in embalming and is said to keep its fragrance for 100 years.

Stockings

The history of the Christmas stocking is wrapped up in the legend of St. Nicholas. As the story goes, St. Nick learned of three poor sisters in need of a lot of money. One night, he tossed a sack of gold for one sister through their window. The next night, he tossed a second sack for the second sister. On the third night, the window was closed, so St. Nicholas dropped the gold down the chimney. The coins fell into the third sister's stocking, which was hanging by the fireplace to dry. The news spread fast, and everyone in town hung up their stockings, hoping for a little something from St. Nick.

A LUMP OF COAL

Anyone who has ever celebrated Christmas—and has ever been a child—has probably been threatened with a lump of coal in their Christmas stocking. Supposedly, it stems from a Sicilian tradition—the legend of La Befana, the "Christmas witch."

On their way to see the Baby Jesus, the wise men stopped at the home of La Befana to ask for directions. They politely invited her to join them, but she said she was too busy—and continued sweeping her steps.

Then La Befana saw a bright star in the sky and thought that she should try to find the men and see the stable after all. She gathered toys and trinkets to give to the Baby Jesus. Unfortunately, she couldn't catch up with the wise men, but every January 6, La Befana sets out on her broom in search of the Christ child. On the way, she leaves toys for all the good children and coal for all the naughty ones. In Italy, parents sometimes slip a little *carbone dolce* (black rock candy or "sweet coal") into their children's stockings as a warning from La Befana.

Gift Giving Customs

*N*o matter when or where you exchange Christmas presents, you probably have your own special way of doing it. Everyone does. Whether your particular family traditions have roots in one of these customs, or this international information inspires you to try something new, it's fun to see how it's done in some faraway places.

In Greece, only children and the poor receive presents on Christmas. On St. Basil's Day (also New Year's Day), some adults exchange gifts.

In Hungary, children place their freshly shined shoes near the door so that little angels may fill them with presents.

In Syria, the youngest camel of the wise men travels through the desert, leaving gifts for good children.

In Germany, Switzerland, and Austria, the *Christkindl*, or the Christ Child—a sweet little angel riding a deer carrying sweets and toys—visits homes on Christmas Eve to deliver presents.

In Poland, children's gifts are said to come from the stars.

In regions of Russia, an old woman named Babushka wanders from house to house on Three Kings Day (January 6) and leaves gifts for good boys and girls. Like La Befana in Italy, she is believed to have been approached by Magi on their way to Bethlehem.

In Puerto Rico, children hide plants and flowers in small boxes under their beds as gifts for the wise men's camels. The kids are rewarded with special presents from the wise men when they pass through on Three Kings Day.

In Search of the Perfect Gift

There's so much pressure to find "the perfect gift," and yet . . . does such a thing even exist? How many hours have you wasted wandering around a store waiting for inspiration to strike? Let's face it, holiday minutes seem to fly by twice as fast as the regular ones, and there are a million better ways to spend them than by browsing a catalog or clearance bin. Besides, how many tie tacks does one guy need?

Ralph Waldo Emerson said, "The only gift is a portion of thyself." And if you ask anyone what their favorite gift of all time has been, you may find they're likely to agree. Most people's prized gifts from past Christmases are small and meaningful—something made by their children, knit or sewn by Grandma, or handed down from a special friend. Of course, we can't give these kinds of special gifts to everyone every year. But you can add a touch of yourself—that certain just-for-you something that your friends and family will really adore.

SOME IDEAS

※ Transfer old home movies to DVD.

※ Make a calendar, coffee mug, or coasters from family photos.

※ Tie-dye t-shirts for the whole group.

※ Make a trail mix of Dad's favorite ingredients.

※ Stencil tote bags or aprons with fun quotations.

※ Make fridge magnets of the kids' school pictures.

※ Personalize blank books for writers in the family.

※ Stamp baby's handprints onto decorative tiles.

※ Monogram note cards on the computer or with a rubber stamp.

※ Make a mixed CD of favorite music.

※ Print a quote book of "Funny Things Your Grandkids Said."

※ Fill a recipe organizer with favorite family recipes.

※ Create a photo album or scrapbook around a certain theme (family trips, sisterly love, etc.)

※ Write and bind a favorite story, such as "How I Met Your Mom" or "The Day You Were Born."

To make gifts really special, let the kids make their own wrapping paper. Spread a roll of kraft paper (brown or white) out on the table. With stamps, markers, stickers, and stencils, let the kids go to town. They'll be really proud to hand-deliver their specially wrapped presents.

Gimme Gimme!

$\mathcal{L}$et's face it, Christmas and kids don't always mix. Here are a few suggestions for countering those "gotta-have-it" Christmas jitters.

TUNE OUT

Try to make more together time and less time in front of the tube. Surveys have shown that 85% of kids get the items for their Christmas lists by watching commercials.

GIVE A LITTLE

Look for this opportunity at work, church, or in the community. If your kids are aware of how less fortunate families celebrate, they may be less inclined to want so much. They'll also enjoy being able to help make another kid happy on Christmas.

ENCOURAGE ENTREPRENEURSHIP

In the months leading up to Christmas, give kids small chores and small allowances (if they don't already get one) and encourage them to use it to buy Christmas gifts for family members. You'll probably find that they're almost as excited to give as to receive.

GREAT EXPECTATIONS?

Keep an open dialog with the wee ones about what they're expecting—and what's realistic. "Wouldn't it be wonderful if Santa brought you three presents! What could you imagine they would be?" A little reality check here and there can avoid a full-blown meltdown on Christmas morning—which can happen when kids' expectations may be impossibly high.

Giving, Family Style

Is your big family putting a big dent in your bank account? Don't get me wrong—exchanging gifts is a time-honored pastime. And it's fun! But there are ways to save some money without sacrificing festivity. Here are a few ideas.

SET A LIMIT

Make everyone pledge to spend no more than a predetermined amount of money. You might also try instituting an age limit, too, if your teenagers can handle it.

GIFTS IN BULK

Give the same gift (with small variations) to each family member. A framed photo of the kids, hot cocoa and personalized mug, socks of their favorite color, etc.

GET CREATIVE

Insist that no gifts may be bought in a store. Those of us who aren't crafty have to get creative. Babysitting, car washes, help painting the house . . . some gifts are worth more than money.

THE GIFT OF TIME

Instead of giving gifts, decide on a family outing everyone will enjoy. A Broadway show? Weekend at the beach? Afternoon at the spa? All good choices! And you'll get the bonus gift of great memories from your time together.

SIMPLE GIFTS

There's a song you may know—an old Shaker hymn, actually: "'Tis a Gift to Be Simple." At Christmastime, when commercials, billboards, and shop windows try to persuade you of all the things you and your loved ones simply can't do without, try to take a deep breath and remember these lyrics. There's something to be said for simplicity. It really can go a long way toward reducing holiday distress—to your bank account, your family, and ultimately, yourself!

Giving Games

$\mathscr{A}$ good, fun game may just pump some life into your next gift-giving gathering. Most of these games work best with adults, but include kids if they understand the just-for-fun spirit of the exchange.

GRAB BAG

A classic. Set a spending limit and have everyone bring a wrapped present. Collect the presents in a large bag and, when it's time, have everyone reach in and pick their present. Try giving the grab bag a theme, like "edibles," "board games," or "gift cards."

PASS IT ON

Everyone brings a wrapped present for this one, too, then stands or sits in a circle. Have someone read aloud a popular Christmas story (*How the Grinch Stole Christmas* is a fun one). Before you start, designate a word that, when read, will signal everyone to pass gifts to the left and another that will signal to pass to the right. (A tip: pick words that appear often, like "Grinch" or "Christmas.") As the book is read, pass gifts accordingly. When the story ends, players keep the gift they're holding.

This game can also be played with a favorite Christmas song. Pick one with a repeating chorus of choice words for an extra good time.

SECRET SANTA

Also known as "Kris Kringle." Ahead of time, have everyone choose a friend or family member's name out of a hat. (Do it at Thanksgiving, when people are likely to be in the same place.) Get the person you've drawn the best gift you can buy for twenty dollars (or whatever dollar amount the group agrees upon). Keep it a secret 'til Christmas—or forever, if you can stand it. (A fun variation: have the recipients guess who their "Secret Santa" is after opening the present. If they guess correctly, they get another small gift.)

This game can also be played for an extended period of time if the players live near one another or don't mind the mail. This way, Secret Santas keep tabs on good boys and girls for several days—or weeks—and leave little rewards for people to find on their pillows, in their pockets, or on their desks at work.

WHITE ELEPHANT

Also known as "Yankee Swap" or "Dirty Christmas," this one isn't ideal for small children. If you've ever played it, you know why.

Set a spending limit and have everyone bring a wrapped, unlabeled present and set it in a designated spot. When everyone's ready, write out on small scraps of paper a number for however many people are playing and have everyone draw a number.

Number 1 goes first by choosing a gift—any gift—and opening it. Number 2 may then choose any gift—including the gift just opened by Number 1. (A nasty trick if Number 1 really liked what she got! But if someone's gift gets taken out from under her, she does get to open another.) Number 3 follows the same rule as Number 2, and so on. At the end, Number 1 gets to go again. (There are a million variations, by the way. Choose the ones that best suit your group.)

This game got its name from an old Burmese custom. In Burma, albino (white) elephants are considered sacred and must be very well taken care of, no matter how much it costs the owner. It's a reference to the impractical, silly, or just plain terrible gifts you might get stuck with while playing this game. Like the giant inflatable palm tree you got last year.

Giving Back

One way of knowing for sure that your gift will be used and appreciated is to give the gift of helping others. Whether you make an outright donation, donate in someone's name, or volunteer your time, you're making a great choice. And that's something to feel good about.

This time of year, lots of charities offer special gift options—so there's bound to be something for everyone on your list. Here are just a few suggestions.

FIRST BOOK · firstbook.org/shop
A great idea for teachers and readers alike. Remember the joy of reading and owning your very first book? Here's an organization with a mission to provide children from low-income families with the same experience. First Book provides brand-new books to children participating in community-based mentoring, tutoring, and family literacy programs. And their site lists fun, reading-related products that support the mission.

A GREATER GIFT · agreatergift.com
Got a world traveler in the family who seems to have everything? A Greater Gift offers fair-trade handcrafts and foods from around the world, promoting living wages, women's rights, and eco-friendly production through their partnerships with small-scale artisan and farmer groups.

SAVE THE WHALES · savethewhales.org
Animal lovers will adore this one. Each whale adoption kit includes an official certificate, newsletter, sticker, and photo of the wild orca you're supporting.

ST. JUDE'S CHILDREN'S RESEARCH HOSPITAL · shop.stjude.org
Honor a cancer survivor, awareness advocate, or healthcare provider with a gift from St. Jude's. You can also purchase meaningful gifts of all kinds through their Hope Catalog, available online and by mail.

If you are still wondering which charity to support, visit justgive.org, where you can browse, search, and find a charity perfectly suited to you and the ones you love.

Every year, we celebrated the Epiphany with family friends. My mother spent all year looking for Christmas cards featuring the wise men, which she'd attach to our gifts. There was always a "king cake" with trinkets and beans baked into it. Each trinket had a little poem attached, written by my mother's friend. But even if you got a bean, you were lucky because you got to wear a cardboard crown and Mardi Gras beads and play the role of one of the wise men. The Epiphany was lots of things to us—a family reunion, a party, another way to celebrate the miracle of Christmas, and also, a way to make the season last a little bit longer. I like to continue the tradition as best I can. On January 6, I give my daughters their last Christmas present: a book, the gift of wisdom.

—Patty Hayden, Bay St. Louis, MS

My Grandmother "Chum" grew up during the depression—and stuffed her children's stockings with a tangerine, a comb . . . and a walnut! We continued the tradition—with a twist. My brothers, cousins, and I would gather all the walnuts we could find and stash them in Chum's bed on Christmas night. We were such naughty kids. She had a sense of humor, though, because she usually just picked up the nuts and put them in our stockings, which made a lot less room for the stuff we really wanted, like candy and toys.

—Karen Swyers, Belmont, MA

Real Traditions

Our favorite family tradition is the night-before-Christmas gift. On Christmas Eve, each member of the family gets to open one present from under the tree. What makes this tradition silly and fun is that my mom chooses which gift, and every year we find the same thing: pajamas! We all wear our new pajamas to bed, and we're not allowed to change out of them on Christmas morning until after we've had breakfast and opened the rest of our gifts. We may have bleary eyes and bedhead, but we all have fresh, new jammies. It's fun.

—Stacey Nichols Kim, Portland, OR

Here Comes Santa Claus

Years ago, on an otherwise humdrum December evening, the phone rang. Everyone in my family stopped what they were doing, and for a magical moment, time stood still as my father's words hung in the air: "Kids . . . Santa's on the phone."

What? Santa? THE Santa?

Time resumed its normal speed about a half second later when my brother, his cheeks flush with excitement, wish list already tripping off his tongue, nearly flattened me on the way to the phone. I, on the other hand, stood frozen, looking for a place to hide. What could I possibly say to Santa Claus, the guy who somehow sees you when you're sleeping, knows when you're awake . . . and once a year judges just how bad or good you've been?

When I was finally coaxed to the phone, Santa asked me in a kind, vaguely familiar voice what I wanted for Christmas. I hesitated, kicking my toe in the carpet and stammering whatever words I could find. This was the moment every child waits for. And as terrified as I was, I didn't want it to end.

Only one man inspires such a mixture of exhilaration, intrigue, and downright frenzy in households around the world. Although his history as a saintly do-gooder may go back as far as the fourth century, the Santa we all know and love is as close and comfortable as our favorite Christmas memories.

From the time he left that sooty note of thanks for the cookies to the year my brother swore he heard him make a pit stop in the bathroom down the hall, Santa has left us so much more over the years than brightly wrapped presents. He's also left us some of the best stories we have to tell—and the reminder of what magical things can happen when we simply believe.

This Christmas Eve, when you and your family hang your stockings with care before settling in for a long winter's nap, prepare for a brush with greatness. Because there's a red-suited renegade out there making his famous midnight ride, just crazy enough to think he can make the world a happier place with a good, generous heart and eight tiny reindeer.

The Story of St. Nick

Santa didn't start his career as a jolly old elf in a red suit, but as a kindhearted bishop in fourth-century Turkey. Nicholas was known so widely for his good works and selfless deeds that he was later granted sainthood. Among his notable acts of kindness was an anonymous gift of gold to a family of three poor girls. In the night, he tossed the gold through their window and it landed in a stocking hung above the fire to dry.

That was just the beginning. For years to come, people told stories of children he'd helped and lives he'd made better. In the twelfth century, French nuns began giving out candy and gifts to children of needy families in honor of his feast day—December 6. The custom soon caught on all across Europe, and rich and poor children alike began finding small gifts left in secret during the night.

By the 1300s, St. Nick had reportedly begun delivering his gifts by climbing down children's chimneys. The Dutch called him *Sinterklaas* and brought his stories and traditions to the New World. There, his name changed slightly to Santa Claus, which is how we know him today.

In 1822, Clement Clarke Moore described Santa's now-famous rosy cheeks and jelly belly in his poem "A Visit From Saint Nicholas" and unknowingly changed the look of Santa Claus forever. In 1869, Thomas Nast, head cartoonist for *Harper's Weekly*, became the first person to paint on the red suit. And Haddon Sundblom's famous Coca-Cola™ ads from the 1930s through 1960s immortalized the white-bearded, black-belted commercial success that Santa is today.

No matter how we see him, Santa's true character remains the same. He may have changed his clothes and gained a few pounds, but he's still the generous, jolly ol' St. Nick we've known for centuries, spreading the spirit of giving wherever he goes.

A Jolly Old Elf

The poem we now know as "'Twas the Night Before Christmas" was first printed in New York's Troy Sentinel newspaper on December 23, 1823. These famous lines made visions of sugarplums dance in readers' heads. It also gave everyone, for the first time, a collective vision of ol' St. Nick himself . . . the twinkly-eyed, cherry-nosed guy we picture when we think of Santa Claus today.

He was dressed all in fur, from his head to his foot,
And his clothes were all tarnished with ashes and soot;
A bundle of toys he had flung on his back,
And he looked like a peddler just opening his pack.
His eyes—how they twinkled! His dimples—how merry!
His cheeks were like roses, his nose like a cherry!
His droll little mouth was drawn up like a bow,
And the beard on his chin was as white as the snow;
The stump of a pipe he held tight in his teeth,
And the smoke it encircled his head like a wreath;
He had a broad face and little round belly
That shook when he laughed, like a bowl full of jelly.
He was chubby and plump, a right jolly old elf,
And I laughed when I saw him, in spite of myself . . .

Dear Santa

A puppy. A bike. A new baby brother . . . Over the years, Santa's heard it all. And sometimes the letters don't stop with a wish list. Kids also write Santa to fess up to bad behavior, to put in a good word for someone else, to ask questions about Rudolph's famous schnoz, and to offer the kind of advice only kids can get away with: "Maybe Mrs. C. shouldn't let you have so many cookies, Santa. Your big belly might get stuck in the chimney."

In order to accommodate the volume of mail he receives each year, Santa has set up alliances with post offices all over the world. Here are a few cities where Santa's mail is received and processed:

North Pole, Alaska, U.S.A.
Santa Claus, Indiana, U.S.A.
The North Pole, Canada
Napapiiri, Finland (at the Arctic Circle)

His Alaska address alone sees 120,000 letters a year, from nearly 30 different countries. The ambitious elves at this P.O. handle 12,000 letters a day during crunch time—and they do their best to answer every one.

The big guy's gone digital, too. At **emailsanta.com**, kids can send him a virtual letter. And he'll write back, quick as a cyberwink.

There Is a Santa Claus!

In 1897, newspaper editor Francis P. Church was handed a letter from an eight-year-old girl with a very important question. Suddenly, the faith of children everywhere was in Church's hands. His reply to Virginia became the most reprinted newspaper editorial of all time—and restored a childlike faith to readers everywhere.

I am 8 years old. Some of my little friends say there is no Santa Claus. Papa says, "If you see it in The Sun it's so." Please tell me the truth; is there a Santa Claus?

—Virginia O'Hanlon

Virginia, your little friends are wrong. They have been affected by the skepticism of a skeptical age. They do not believe except what they see. . . .

Yes, Virginia, there is a Santa Claus.

He exists as certainly as love and generosity and devotion exist, and you know that they abound and give to your life its highest beauty and joy. Alas! How dreary would be the world if there were no Santa Claus! It would be as dreary as if there were no Virginias. There would be no childlike faith then, no poetry, no romance to make tolerable this

existence. We should have no enjoyment, except in sense and sight. The external light with which childhood fills the world would be extinguished.

Not believe in Santa Claus! You might as well not believe in fairies! You might get your papa to hire men to watch in all the chimneys on Christmas Eve to catch Santa Claus, but even if they did not see Santa Claus coming down, what would that prove? Nobody sees Santa Claus, but that is no sign that there is no Santa Claus. The most real things in the world are those that neither children nor men can see. Did you ever see fairies dancing on the lawn? Of course not, but that's no proof that they are not there. Nobody can conceive or imagine all the wonders there are unseen and unseeable in the world. . . .

No Santa Claus? Thank God—he lives, and he lives forever. A thousand years from now, Virginia, nay ten times ten thousand years from now, he will continue to make glad the heart of childhood.

—The New York Sun, 1897

Pictures With Santa

*M*ost of the time, you don't even get a glimpse of Santa's sleigh on Christmas Eve. He sneaks in and out, quiet as a mouse.

Luckily, in 1890, a man named James Edgar started the tradition of the "department store Santa," allowing us to visit Santa and his elves and get a little glimpse of the North Pole right in our own neighborhood. All it takes is a few dollars and a pinch of patience—and you can deliver your Christmas wish list in person.

SANTA STRESS?

Every department store Santa knows that two out of three little ones are likely to burst into tears at the mere sight of him. If one such Santa-shy youngster belongs to you, don't be alarmed. There's always next year. As for this year, there are lots of other photo opportunities. You may just have to make them yourself.

ROLE REVERSAL

Find a plush Santa doll and put him in *the little one's* lap. It'll be cute, creative, and unexpected.

SANTA HATS FOR EVERYONE

There are few times a year when the whole family has an excuse to do weird things, like wear bright red stocking caps in public. You can buy inexpensive Santa hats just about anywhere. And everyone can decorate a hat with their own personal flair.

PLAY DRESS UP

They'll have fun playing holiday hero. Dress the kids as Santa and take them to a nursing home to share candy with the residents, or let the dog pull them around the neighborhood in a wagon "sleigh."

SNAP A SHOT WITH RUDOLPH

Find a nearby petting zoo in your community that keeps reindeer—or any kind of deer—who like to have their picture taken. The kids will get to go to the zoo, feed and pet the animals, and you'll get your keepsake. It's win-win!

POSTCARD FROM THE POLE

Make the next time it snows a family photo opportunity. Paint "The North Pole" on plywood or corrugate cardboard, attach it to a long stick (a broom handle will work just fine), and take your kids' Christmas card picture out in the snowy drifts. Try a postcard format and write "Wish you were here!" or "Greetings from your favorite elves!" across the bottom. For extra interest and lots of laughs, get each kid a pointy hat and pair of elf ears.

Interested in playing Santa? You might consider going back to school. Santa school! Founded in 1937, The Charles W. Howard Santa Claus School in Midland, Michigan, is the oldest school dedicated to the art of portraying Santa Claus. Mr. Howard was technical adviser for the Christmas classic *Miracle on 34th Street*, and his school teaches courses in everything from the history of St. Nick to wigs, makeup, and beards.

Santas Around the World

TRANSLATION SERVICE

It's true that the guy in red is loved by children the world over. So it may not come as a surprise that he answers to a different name in each country he visits. In case you ever find yourself traveling at Christmastime and looking for the local Kris Kringle, you'll be glad to have the following list of Santa pseudonyms.

DESTINATION	SANTA
Armenia	Gaghant Baba
Australia	Kris Kringle
Brazil	Papai Noel
Bulgaria	Diado Coleda
Chile	Viejo Pascuero
China	Dun Che Lao Ren
Finland	Joulupukki
France	Père Noël
Greece	Nikolaos
Hawaii	Kanakaloka
Italy	Babbo Natale
Japan	Santa Kurohsu
Norway	Julenissen
Slovenia	Bozicek
Spain	Papa Noel
United Kingdom	Father Christmas
Yugoslavia	Deda Mraz

The Santa Squad

$\mathcal{B}$eing Santa is such a big job that he calls on helpers all around the world to assist with his annual delivery of Yuletide cheer. Check out a few of Santa's closest Christmas compadres.

* *Sinterklaas* arrives in Holland on St. Nicholas Eve (December 5). Children leave wooden shoes filled with hay and carrots (for the white horse *Sinterklaas* rides) by the fireplace. If they're good, they'll awake to find their shoes filled with candies, nuts, and small toys.

* In Russia, children wait for *Ded Moroz* (Grandfather Frost), who delivers toys door-to-door from a horse-drawn sleigh. He is said to live deep in the Russian woods and is often accompanied on his annual visit by a young woman known as the Snow Maiden.

* In many countries, including Spain and Mexico, children wait for the *reyes magos*, or three kings, to deliver gifts on Three Kings Day (January 6). Children often leave offerings of food and drink for the visitors and the camels they ride.

* A winged baby called *Cristkindl*, symbolizing the Christ child, arrives in Austria and Germany to deliver gifts and decorate the Christmas tree. The tinkling of a silver bell announces the arrival of *Cristkindl* and his band of angels.

* There are thirteen gift givers in Iceland called *jólasveinar*, or "Yuletide Lads." Every year, they come to town one by one to give away gifts and sweets—and to wreak havoc on Christmas preparations! The lads have been blamed for everything from stealing food to slamming doors. Starting December 13th, children put a shoe on the windowsill at night. If they've been good, a *jólasveinar* leaves a little gift. If they've been bad, they get a potato.

* In Australia, it's Santa, or Kris Kringle, who does the Christmas Eve deliveries. But when he arrives, he trades in his eight flying reindeer (who have had a very long flight) for another team of helpers: eight white kangaroo!

The Midnight Flight Crew

$\mathcal{B}$elieve it or not, nobody knew the names of Santa's reindeer until "A Visit From Saint Nicholas" was printed in 1823. But thanks to Clement Clarke Moore's clever rhymes, now almost anyone can recite them by heart.

More rapid than eagles, his coursers they came,
And he whistled and shouted and called them by name:
Now, Dasher! Now, Dancer! Now, Prancer and Vixen!
On, Comet! On, Cupid! On, Dunder and Blixem!
To the top of the porch! To the top of the wall!
Now dash away! Dash away! Dash away all!

Though the author originally used *Dunder* and *Blixem*, the Dutch words for thunder and lightning, with time we've adopted *Donner* and *Blitzen*, their German synonyms.

THE REINDEER REPORT

※ Male reindeer shed their antlers every year long before December 25. Females keep theirs until at least January. (So if you ever catch a real glimpse at Santa's sleigh, you'll be able to identify Vixen and the other does right away.)

※ The North Pole is Santa's Christmas post, but the reindeer most likely spend the rest of the year hanging around Lapland, Finland, near the Korvatunturi mountain. How do they pass the time? Probably playing reindeer games.

※ Rudolph was not part of the original great eight. He joined the team in 1939, when Robert L. May published his story for Montgomery Ward.

※ When you see them pawing at the ground with their hooves, it doesn't necessarily mean Santa's reindeer are waiting for him to get the show on the road. They're probably pawing through the snow to find lichen to eat—a favorite mossy reindeer snack.

※ Reindeer weigh up to 250 pounds and can carry a load that weighs as much as they do. So eight reindeer could pull a sleigh with a literal ton of toys in it. Not bad for one night's work!

Santa's Little Helpers

They work all year to make the toys for little boys and girls all around the world. Elves may just be the hardest workers in history—that we know. But here are some things about Santa's little friends that you may not know.

* Elves were first spotted in northern Europe and Scandinavia, where they lived in trees and were mistaken as tree spirits.

* According to "'Twas the Night Before Christmas," Santa himself is an elf!

* Elves have also been called pixies, dryads, fairies, brownies, and huldefolk. They're cousins to Leprechauns. They're generally kind creatures, with a mysterious and magical knack for knowing whether or not a person has been behaving.

* Finnish writer Zacharias Topelius, Swedish poet Victor Rydberg, and children's author Caroline H. Butler seemed to know the inside story back in the late 1800s. Each of them published works that revealed how elves' true purpose was not to haunt trees but to help Father Christmas.

Tracking Santa

In 1955, a Sears Roebuck & Co. store ran an advertisement encouraging children to call Santa on a special holiday hotline. One problem: they accidentally misprinted the phone number. As a result, children who called the number didn't reach Santa, but Colonel Harry Shoup, Commander in Chief of the Continental Air Defense Command (CONAD) in Colorado Springs, CO. But the quick-thinking colonel didn't miss a beat. Soon he had his staff checking for signs of Santa on their radar data and sharing that information with all the kids who called in. And just like that . . . a tradition was born.

CONAD joined forces with Canada in 1958 and created NORAD (North American Aerospace Defense Command), which now handles all Santa tracking on Christmas Eve. The men and women who work at NORAD personally answer children's calls—as well as calls from media stations around the world needing updates on Santa's location.

Using sophisticated radar, satellites that detect infrared signals given off by Rudolph's nose, specially placed "Santa Cams," and even a jet-fighter escort, NORAD is able to follow Santa as he makes his way south from the North Pole. Now if they could only predict what he'll be leaving under your Christmas tree . . .

Too cold out to watch the sky for your own UFS (Unidentified Flying Sleigh) sighting? Stay in where it's warm and track Santa's flight around the world with NORAD's live video updates at noradsanta.org.

When I was little, I'd come downstairs to find not only a plethora of presents, but also a thank-you note to me from Santa for the cookies and milk I'd left (since I was the youngest in the family and the only one who still believed in the old guy). The thing is—he always misspelled my name! And it wasn't some clever attempt at authenticity on the part of my parents . . . it was because my grandma was always the one commissioned to write the note. And, God love her, either she wasn't used to staying up that late or someone spiked the eggnog—because she never remembered that my name began with a C and not an S!

—Chandra Blackwell, Atlanta, GA

On Christmas Eve after the children were in bed, my husband would climb up on the roof and stomp around pretending to be Santa Claus. But that was only the start. He also dangled a flashlight wrapped in red paper against their bedroom windows and added sound effects with jingling bells and generous "Ho-Ho-Hos." But the best were the ashes he would scatter from the fireplace to the Christmas tree! The kids are grown, but he's got the ladder all set to go for when we have our first grandchild.

—Beth Fonville, Killeen, TX

Real Traditions

Every Christmas Eve, my father's fire company chauffeured Santa Claus through town in a bright red engine so the kids could get a peek at him before he hopped on his sleigh and did his thing. Once, after dinner, my brother and I heard the siren from Dad's fire engine. Peering from the window, we saw Santa climb out of the truck—with my father right behind him. That was so cool. My dad knew Santa! And brought him to us! I'm in the fire department now, and alongside my dad, I help bring Santa and Mrs. Claus to a new generation of firefighter's kids. I spend the week before Christmas collecting addresses and bedtimes from each firefighter. Then we spend Christmas Eve putting awestruck expressions on little kids' faces. I don't think it'll ever get old.

—Bill Madden, Oceanside, NY

Christmas Goodies

Sugar cookies. Homemade candies. Hot cocoa by the mug-full. 'Tis the season, all right . . . for stretchy pants!

From the scrumptious sweets sprinkled throughout the season to the sumptuous Christmas feast, no other season so heartily dedicates itself to such pure, unabashed indulgence. And I, for one, am completely on board with that.

As tantalizing as this smorgasbord of gourmet goodies is, you have to admit Christmas has long been a holiday of food extremes. On one hand, you have platefuls of some of the all-time greatest hits—those comfort foods that are as familiar as family itself: mouthwatering ham and turkey, creamy mashed potatoes, all kinds of delectable pies. On the other hand, you've got some real quirks. You know the ones: figgy pudding, mincemeat pie, rumballs. You may only see them once a year, but—like certain relatives—it just wouldn't be Christmas without them.

We've all got our own tastes, our own ideas of what's classically Christmas—no matter how unusual they might seem to others. But whatever you're serving, and whether it's for collective enjoyment or collective commiseration ("Is that the same fruitcake from last year?"), the *really* great thing about holiday goodies is that they bring people together.

If you're skeptical of this theory, put a big plate of cookies in a common area at work and see how quickly it draws people away from their computers. Or watch as all your holiday party guests inevitably migrate to the welcoming warmth of the kitchen. People can't resist a tasty tidbit or two, especially when it's served up with some genuine holiday cheer.

So ladies and gents, start your ovens. Because if there's one tradition that's a sure recipe for holiday happiness, it's food. Whatever you're fixing, here's hoping that warm, homemade memories are coming right up.

Festive Favorites

CANDY CANES

Legend has it that in 1670, a German choirmaster gave candy sticks bent to resemble shepherd's crooks to his young charges in order to keep them quiet during the Christmas service. But it wasn't until the early 1900s that the canes were made with red and white stripes and snappy peppermint flavor.

Each year, more than a billion and a half candy canes are made. Most are manufactured by machine, but some are still pulled and twisted by hand, like the specialty candy canes at Hammonds Candies (hammondscandies.com).

Holiday hustle and bustle got you a little worn out? Studies show that the scent of peppermint perks up the senses. (Like smelling salts, but with a tastier payoff.)

FRUITCAKE!

The fruitcake dates back to the Middle Ages. Early versions, such as Scottish Black Bun, bride cakes, and plum cakes, were luxuries reserved for special occasions. In fact, they were even banned at one time throughout Europe for being "sinfully rich."

Fruitcakes began being ceremoniously saved during the 1700s. At the end of the harvest, a fruitcake would be baked with the season's nuts and fruits. Then, in hopes of blessing the next harvest, the cake would be saved and eaten the *following* year.

The oldest fruitcake? No one really knows where it is, but The Collins Street Bakery in Corsicana, Texas (collinstreet.com), just may be the oldest fruitcake bakery. They have been making the tasty cakes from the same recipe since 1896.

If you'd rather wear your fruitcake than eat it, visit ilovefruitcake.com and check out their t-shirt collection. Proclaim your love for the tasty treat with "Nuts about Fruitcake" or "I'm with Fruitcake." Or give one to a fruitcake-loving friend.

Don't know what to do with that fruitcake Aunt Mildred sent you? Consider the Great Fruitcake Toss. Held every January in Manitou Springs, Colorado, this competition involves tossing fruitcakes (by hand), launching fruitcakes (by catapult), racing fruitcakes (fruitcakes on wheels), and an art show (exhibiting, of course, fruitcakes).

NOW BRING US SOME FIGGY PUDDING

Actually, figgy pudding is more like a cake than a pudding. It's been around since the 15th century, but was most popular during the late 19th century. There may be several reasons it didn't stand the test of time. First, some of the ingredients (figs and spices) are expensive in most places this time of year. Second, it's loaded with saturated fat. And finally, you have to "steam" it for about four hours before serving—which means those folks who won't go until they get some may just have to stay awhile.

EGG-NOGGIN

Like many of our old Christmas traditions, eggnog has a colorful, if murky, history. It's related to the kind of milk and wine punches that were made long ago in Europe. Once it arrived in the New World though, Americans preferred to spike it with rum. In colonial days, rum was commonly called "grog." Some think "egg and grog" may have been shortened over time to "eggnog." Others say the drink gets its name from "noggin," a wooden tavern mug. The real story might be a combination of both versions, making the drink "egg and grog in a noggin." Now that's a mouthful.

In the 1800s, few city folks had access to fresh eggs and milk (since refrigeration wasn't what it is now), so a batch of eggnog had to be consumed immediately. It quickly became a beverage best enjoyed with large groups of thirsty friends. And so the party drink was born.

George Washington was such a fan of eggnog that he invented his own recipe containing four kinds of liquor, which he'd serve only to his bravest Chrismas guests.

International Delights

GLÖGG

The Swedish version of mulled wine, glögg is found throughout Scandanavia. It's usually served warm during the holidays. Glögg may or may not contain wine, but it always has lots of spice. In fact, some Scandinavians claim it's the best treatment for the common cold.

FEAST OF THE SEVEN FISHES

This is a tradition from southern Italy. Some say the number seven stands for the seven sacraments of the Catholic Church. Others claim it's for the seven days in which God created the earth or the seven days it took Mary and Joseph to travel to Bethlehem. Still others say it's for the seven hills of Rome.

The truth is, many Italian families serve less than seven fish. And many serve a good deal more. Most holiday recipes include *baccalà* (dried cod), and many desserts feature the traditional *strufoli*—pea-sized pastries flavored with honey.

LA PIÑATA

Though it's originally from Italy, the art of the piñata has been perfected by Mexico. A favorite part of the Christmas celebration for the young and young at heart, piñatas were traditionally made out of clay pots and decorated with crepe paper. Today's piñatas are made out of much safer papier mâché and cardboard. The traditional design is a star, and the traditional filling is *colaciones*— cooked candies with mustard in the middle. Today, families can choose from a huge variety of piñata shapes and fillings.

WASSAIL

Modern reproductions of this traveling British beverage resemble hot cider. Historically, it was probably more like beer—with lots of other ingredients and sometimes topped with slices of toast.

Here's a recipe from 1633: "Boil three pints of ale; beat six eggs, the whites and yolks together; set both to the fire in a pewter pot; add roasted apples, sugar, beaten nutmegs, cloves, and ginger; and, being well-brewed, drink it while hot." (Yum!)

THIRTEEN DESSERTS

In France, the Christmas grocery budget is about equal to the budget for presents. Traditionally, families attend midnight mass and return home for le réveillon—the Christmas Eve "wake-up" meal. The menu varies, but is likely to include foie gras, escargot, oysters, and goose.

In Provence, and across the south of France, there are usually thirteen desserts—one for each of those who attended the Last Supper. This menu varies, too, but will probably feature a variety of nuts, candied fruits, fruit tarts, flavored nougats, and *la pompe à l'huile* (a cake named "the oil pump").

SHARING PEACE

It's tradition in Poland for the extended family to gather for Christmas dinner. And before the meal is served, the oldest guest distributes the "peace wafer"—a small white wafer blessed by the church and decorated with scenes from the nativity. Each person at the table shares his or her wafer as a token of friendship and peace.

Christmas Cookies

This is a tradition that seems more personal than any. No matter your heritage, your memories of favorite Christmas cookies probably depend on the kinds of cookies your mother or grandmother baked—or bought.

The history of the "Christmas cookie" is elusive, at best. Historically, where there was celebration, there were sweets. And where there were sweets, there were cookies.

Here's a look at the history of the cookie as we know it.

It's derived from the Dutch word *koekje*—"little cake." According to food historians, cookies were first used as test cakes: a small amount of cake batter was baked to test the recipe and oven temperature.

The earliest ones date back to 7th century Persia. Not surprising, since Persia was one of the first countries to produce sugar. By the end of the 14th century, street vendors in Paris were selling thin, sweet "wafers," and cookbooks were filled with the recipes. During the 17th and 18th centuries, baking was a strict business in Europe. Bakers had to complete years of apprenticeship. But by the time the Industrial Revolution came along, technology helped make sweet and savory biscuits available for mass consumption.

CHOCOLATE CHIP

The first chocolate chip cookies were invented in 1937 by Ruth Graves Wakefield at the Toll House Inn in Whitman, Massachusetts. (The chocolate chip cookie was designated the state cookie of Massachusetts in 1997.)

BROWNIES

Many believe that the brownie is the result of a delicious accident. A preoccupied chef neglected to add baking powder to his chocolate cake batter. In 1897, the Sears, Roebuck & Co. catalog published the first recipe and soon after, offered the first boxed mix.

MACAROONS

These coconut cookies originated in an Italian monastery, where Carmelite nuns took asylum during the French Revolution. They paid for their housing in macaroons—the brothers' favorite treat.

SNICKERDOODLES

There was no "cookie chapter" in early American cookbooks. Instead, what we know today as cookies were listed at the end by such names as "jumbles," "plunkets," and "cry babies." Snickerdoodles come from this New England tradition—along with other whimsically named cookies like graham jakes, jolly boys, tangle breeches, and kinkawoodles.

GINGERBREAD

It was Germany who shared the gingerbread house tradition with America. No one really knows which came first—the gingerbread house or the story of the gingerbread house (as in "Hansel and Gretel"). Either way, edible abodes first gained popularity in the early 1800s.

The first gingerbread man is credited to Queen Elizabeth I, who liked to charm important visitors with gingerbread likenesses of themselves.

Favorite Cookies

A common Christmastime scene: counter-top, rolling pin, mom, and elated children covered in powdery white. Any minute now the oven will ding and rows of golden holiday shapes will emerge, hot and puffy. Spatulas will scrape across Teflon, and the tasty gems slide onto wire racks. Then, we wait for that first oven-warm bite.

Many of us have favorite cookie-making memories like this. And certainly all of us have a favorite cookie. While some like to stick to that tried-and-true, handed-down recipe, others are always looking for something new and exciting to try. And some of us buy the premixed and molded dough from the freezer section. But no matter how we bake them, we all agree: cookies are a delicious part of Christmas.

According to a survey by Smuckers, here are America's favorite five:

Sugar cutouts	50%
Shortbread or butter cookies	46%
Peanut butter kiss cookies	36%
Gingerbread cookies	30%
Pecan balls	29%

Smart Cookies

*E*ating cookies is always easy. Baking them isn't. Here are some things you can do to simplify the cookie-making process.

✳ Make a double batch of cookie dough, spoon the extra balls onto a cookie sheet and stick them in the freezer. In a couple of hours you can transfer them to freezer bags and store them for the next time you've got a hankering for homemade cookies.

✳ If you've got little guys with short attention spans, bake cookies ahead of time and get all the decorating ingredients ready before you invite the wee ones to help.

✳ Have a cookie swap early in the holidays, to share the sweetness. That way everyone's got plenty of variety for the whole holiday season. Or at least the next week or so.

✳ Keep moist and chewy cookies soft by storing them in an airtight container with a slice of bread. Replace the slice often. For crisp cookies, tin canisters work best.

✳ Use store-bought dough if you're pressed for time. Better yet, find some neighborhood kids who are selling cookie dough as a fundraiser. You'll get delicious cookies and feel good about helping a worthy cause.

A Bite for Blitzen

Sure, we all know Santa's favorite midnight snack: cookies and milk. But what about a little treat for his faithful reindeer crew? Here's a recipe they're known to gobble up: one cup oatmeal plus one tablespoon glitter. For a whimsical gift for little ones, mix it together in a mason jar and attach the following poem.

Cookies are for Santa,
but don't forget his crew.
The reindeer like a mid-flight snack
to munch and crunch on, too.
So sprinkle this outside
and as it sparkles moonlight-bright,
the reindeer will lead Santa
right to you on Christmas night!

Each year, through Heifer International, I buy an animal for a needy community. Then I make cookies in the shape of the animal I chose. I print out a little gift insert (from the Heifer Web site) and wrap it all in a small box. It's a great gift for coworkers, neighbors, gift exchanges, or anyone who already has enough stuff. Next year I'm thinking of making gingerbread-house cookies along with a donation to Habitat for Humanity. I can't wait.

—Jennifer Zelanzy, Los Angeles, CA

My mom organizes a fabulous Christmas meal for the whole family, which always includes a little menu listing all the foods she's serving. But the really special part is how she personalizes it. Next to each dish, she explains who made it or where it came from ("Lady Diana's Pumpkin Pie," "Dave's Homemade Mashed Potatoes," "Turkey Gravy à la Jar"). She's kept every menu—and looking back on the collection is a great way to remember not only the bounty of food we ate each year but also the wonderful people who celebrated the holiday with us.

—Chelsea Fogleman, Overland Park, KS

Real Traditions

With granddaughters aged 10, 8, and 2, I've always found gingerbread houses a bit tricky. So I came up with an easy and fun alternative: sugar-cube houses! We use frosting to cement the "bricks" together and all kinds of candy for decor. Every year I can see a big difference in the girls' care and style—and the amount of candy they eat before getting it on the house.

—Sandra Willis, Lawton, MI

Gatherings

Faithful friends who are dear to us
gather near to us once more . . .

*N*othing says "it's Christmas" quite like a house buzzing with unpredictable relatives, rambunctious kids, roaming pets, the common cold, and—with any luck—enough laughter to make it all worthwhile.

Whether your idea of togetherness this time of year is cramming as many relatives as you can into every inch of space under one roof or simply enjoying a small seasonal get-together with friends, Christmas is the perfect time for gathering. As the days grow darker and winter's cold sets in, being with and celebrating your favorite people is a surefire way to make spirits bright.

One of my favorite traditions I picked up from my friend Janneke. In the Netherlands, her place of birth, families and friends traditionally gather on December 5, St. Nicholas Eve. Janneke tells me there's no agenda other than being together with loved ones, no big expectations other than the possibility of a little treat in your shoes (whether they're wooden or not) at the end of the night. I must say, the low-maintenance side of me found this concept very attractive.

So I've adapted the tradition myself over the years, hosting friends and loved ones in my own home that evening. I provide the cocoa bar, festive music, and cozy fireside seating while everyone else removes their shoes and shares a plate of their favorite cookies. Before they leave, if they've been good, guests find a little memento in their sneakers.

In the wide spectrum of holiday parties, mine is certainly about as far as you can get from the lavish galas of those more socially talented than I. But somehow it suits everyone in my little circle of friends, giving us a great excuse to enjoy tasty treats, bright conversation, and a cozy little respite from the rest of the holiday hubbub.

Whatever your party-hosting habits, the point is simply to take a break from the daily grind to enjoy how much fun a little time with your favorite people can be. And if everything goes right, which is really much more likely than it sometimes may seem—there may come a moment when you look quietly around at all those faces you've come to know and love, counting them as one of the truest blessings of Christmas.

Parties With Purpose

It's easy to find reasons to celebrate at Chrismas. But sometimes it can be a real challenge to actually find the time to do it.

Here's an idea: try multitasking. If you're a mom, it should come easy to you. Plan your party in such a way that you can also cross off an item on your Christmas to do list. Here are some ideas.

TREE TRIMMING

A fantastic idea for a young couple with only a few items of Christmas decor. Set up your tree, offer cocktails and cocoa, and ask everyone to bring something for the tree—ornaments, garland, a star. If you have the time to prepare a little favor for each of your guests (a personalized ornament? martini glass?), you can cross their names off your Christmas shopping list.

You can also choose to make ornaments instead of having folks bring them. Try painting plain glass globes or decorating gingerbread men. Stringing popcorn is always good for conversation, since it literally brings people close together.

MANY-COURSE MEAL

OK, so you don't get much out of this one except a great meal—and a lot of fun. This works best with neighbors, since the premise is to start the party with appetizers at one person's house, move on to the next for the entrée, and to another's for dessert. But you can stretch the meal out as long as possible by adding a cocktail hour, soup or salad course, after-dinner drinks . . . it's up to you and your group of traveling hostesses.

IT'S A WRAP

This get-together will really cut down on wrapping time come the wee hours of Christmas Eve. Have everyone bring their own roll of tape, a pair of scissors, wrapping paper, plus a little extra in the way of ribbons and bows. And don't forget the gifts! If everyone uses a little of everyone else's supplies, you'll wind up with piles of perfectly eclectic presents. (Here's a tip: provide lots of napkins with whatever snacks you're serving so no one smudges their beautiful wrappings.)

Party Tips

It's an unfortunate truth. Parties are work. But that shouldn't stop you from having one. With a little preparation and a little luck, you can throw a stress-free party. Even at Christmas. Our first suggestion is to welcome the unexpected. (It will show up anyway, so you might as well invite it.) Here are a few more tips.

PREPARING

Send out invitations four weeks before the event. Ask for regrets only to cut down on the number of phone calls you'll receive.

Write lists and stick to them. Make them on the computer so you can print out another one when you lose the first.

Shop for nonperishable supplies at least two weeks ahead of time. If you need a specific item, call the store before you venture out on a wild goose chase.

Don't clean house the day of the party. De-clutter only. Your guests are your friends! No one will care whether you can eat off the floor. No one ever does that anyway.

DECORATING

Choose a theme: red, white, red and green, trees, snowflakes, etc. It'll help you narrow your focus and spend less money on decorations.

Keep the lighting subdued (20 watts are nice). You'll love the cozy mood and your house will look better than ever.

Candles add warmth. But make sure the scent isn't overpowering—and steer clear of pillars and tapers, especially in the company of kids.

FOOD

Go with something foolproof. You don't want to worry about ruining a new recipe. If it's an option, order in.

A little garnish goes a long way. Try fresh herbs, cranberries, and marshmallows (but not in the same dish).

Refill serving dishes often so guests don't feel guilty about taking the last piece.

Go for seconds. It'll set a good example.

Kids' Party Games

Whether your holiday party is kid-exclusive or not, there's no denying it: kids love games. A few of these will really make a splash at your next gathering. With a few variations, they're suitable for game-loving grown-ups, too.

PIN THE NOSE ON THE REINDEER

A Christmasy take on the donkey game. Draw an outline of a reindeer on a large piece of construction paper. Get a few sheets of red circular stickers from your local office supply store. Blindfold and turn the kids three times, then let them go wobbling forth.

CANDY CANE RELAY

Divide the kids into equal-sized groups and space everyone out. The starting kid hangs a candy cane from his index finger and walks (not runs) it to the next player in line. They have to pass the cane from one player to the next—using only their index fingers. (You can't play this game without breaking a few candy canes, so have extras on hand.)

WINTER FREEZE

Collect the kids' favorite holiday music and clear away the furniture. Appoint someone to be the DJ. Their job is to start the music and every thirty seconds or so, stop it and call out "Freeze!" You can eliminate players who don't quite freeze in time—or you can just make it a friendly dance-a-thon.

UNWRAP IT!

Wrap a small gift (CD, DVD, candy bar, etc.). Then put this gift in a larger box, wrap it, and continue two or three times. Get a winter coat, scarf, a hat, and a pair of mittens. Give each child a number and sit them in a circle around the box and clothes. Call out a number randomly. That player has to run up, put on all the clothes, and try to unwrap the present. After twenty seconds, call another number. Hopefully, you'll have the present unwrapped by the end of the party. (If you've got a particularly dexterous group, use duct tape instead of regular tape and oven mitts instead of mittens.)

Gatherings around the World

Nearly 60 million people hit the road for the holidays. Some go a couple of miles to Grandma's house. Some go halfway around the world. Every person has his or her own ideal way of getting people together. Here are some gathering traditions from five places across the globe.

CANADA

In Northern Canada, the Inuit people participate in *Sinck Tuck,* a big party with dancing and gift giving. One village invites another and, the next year, the visiting village returns the favor by hosting the party themselves. The villagers arrive by sled, the dances last for days, and the party goes on for as long as the hosting village can keep it going.

AUSTRALIA

In the southern hemisphere, Christmas comes in the summertime. And in Australia, it's not unusual for the day to reach 100 degrees. So it's common for many Australians to have a picnic dinner—or to head for the beach. Over 40,000 people gather on the half mile of sand at Bondi Beach, where Santa is likely to arrive by boat—or by surfboard!

ISRAEL

On Christmas Eve in Bethlehem, residents and tourists crowd the doorways of the Church of the Nativity (and some stand on the roof) to watch the annual procession of churchmen, government officials, and policemen on Arabian horses. They enter the church and place an ancient figure of the Baby Jesus near the very site where he was born.

SCOTLAND

The Scottish Christmas celebration is usually rather quiet. They reserve their merriment for *Hogmanay,* New Year's Eve. The central theme is warm hospitality, the welcoming of friends and strangers, often sealed with a New Year's kiss. The traditional ceremony included roaring bonfires, blazing barrels of tar, tossing torches, and men dressed up in cattle hides. These customs are still practiced in smaller Scottish villages, though the party in Edinburgh includes a torchlight procession and, afterwards, a magical fireworks display.

The tradition of "First Footing," which is still rather common, says the first person to enter the house determines the family's luck for the following year. Ideally, the first foot belongs to a tall, dark male bearing gifts—hopefully whiskey, coal, small cakes, or a coin. (It's believed to be a throwback to Scotland's Viking days, when a blond stranger at your doorstep was bad news.)

GREECE

In Greece, families gather to celebrate the season, but so do the *Killantzaroi*—a group of goblins, or sprites, who appear on the twelve days between Christmas and January 6. According to legend, they come from the center of the earth and sneak into people's homes through their chimneys. Together, they wreak lots of havoc—souring the milk, snuffing candles, hiding socks and shoes, etc. To keep these unwelcome guests away, Greek families keep the fireplace blazing day and night throughout the twelve days of Christmas.

The Twelfth Day

*J*ust when you've finally committed to taking down the Christmas lights and droopy tree and packing up your memories of Christmas past, remember: there are twelve days of Christmas! Technically, you have through January 6 to enjoy all the season has to offer.

The Twelfth Day is celebrated in many parts of the world and is often as important as Christmas itself. It's believed to be the day the three wise men arrive in Bethlehem—one of the most important gatherings of the season! The holiday has lots of names: the Feast of the Epiphany and Three Kings' Day are just a couple.

Many countries celebrate the Epiphany with food and gifts. A popular Hispanic tradition is to serve the *rosca de reyes*, a crown-shaped sweet bread decorated with candied fruits to resemble jewels. Before baking, one or more tiny baby-shaped charms are hidden in the dough. Whoever gets a piece containing a charm wins a coveted prize—the chance to host another party on or before February 2!

The Twelfth Night

*F*or some, this is simply the same holiday as the Twelfth Day. But in medieval Europe, it was something else entirely. During a winter festival known as the "Feast of Fools," commoners could enjoy a kind of mock role-reversal with the nobility. One bean and one pea were baked into a special "king cake," or *galette des rois*. The man who found the bean became king, the woman who found the pea became queen, and together they enjoyed a reign of "misrule"—lots of merriment, masquerades, and goofy behavior—until the end of the winter festival on January 6.

The Epiphany is also the official start to Carnival, the season between Christmas and Lent. This festive time is celebrated in many places with parties, parties, and more parties . . . the most jubilant of which usually occur during the last days leading up to Mardis Gras, French for "Fat Tuesday."

When I was little, our entire family gathered for Christmas Eve. My parents set up their living room with individual round tables with red tablecloths, like a cozy little restaurant. The television was always tuned in to the Yule log with Christmas carols playing. And after the seven-fish dinner, we played our own version of "The Gong Show," with my grandmothers in charge of the gong. We'd all take turns standing in front of the fireplace telling jokes, singing, dancing, and laughing, laughing, laughing! My father always ended the show singing "O Holy Night," with this one high note that human ears couldn't hear—except on Christmas.

—Diane Albergo, Long Beach, NY

For the past thirteen years, a group of our friends have gotten together for a "Christmas in October" party. It seemed every year we had such trouble finding a time in December when we were all available, so we decided to simply move the party up a couple of months. The host usually does some form of holiday decoration (which is always fun in October—one year I was scolded by the subdivision board president for putting up lights!). We also have a white elephant gift exchange that has grown to include our children as they've gotten older. Certain presents get passed from year to year. There's one awful mirror that someone usually hides in the home of the host for them to find later on.

—Tim Staley, Lenexa, KS

Real Traditions

Since my wife serves in the military, we've had to get used to spending holidays stationed a long way from our loved ones. Fortunately, we have a group of good friends who are in the same boat—and have become a surrogate family of sorts. We've made a tradition of spending Christmas together, enjoying games and a small gift exchange. For the meal, many of us contribute a dish that's a traditional part of our families' celebrations back home. This year I baked my grandmother's legendary pumpkin pie (which was delicious, if I do say so myself). The togetherness is great. And even better—it gives us all a taste of home.

—Larry Okoniewski, Tamuning, Guam

Winter Wonderland

Some of my most cozy-warm memories have been snowy afternoons at my grandparents' place. As kids, my brother and I would hit the slopes of the pasture behind their house, rocketing downhill on the same old wooden sleds my dad had growing up. There were contests involving who could go the farthest and—when Grandma wasn't looking—who could survive the suicidal sled jumps my brother would build on the sly.

Even as we got older, it was an unspoken tradition among our circle of friends to "meet at the pasture" on snow days. We'd sled or battle it out with snowball fights for hours before coming in to the warmth of a good fire, good friends, and mugs of hot cocoa with little white marshmallows bobbing on top.

I know, for many of us, Christmas has become a season of obligations and responsibilities. But sometimes in the middle of all of that, a little gift from heaven arrives in the form of a whisper-soft snowfall. And you and I would probably be wise to stop, hold out our mittened hands, and accept it.

After all, the best winter days remind us of something pretty important: every once in a while, it's all right to simply have fun. To put down the to do list and pick up a snowball. To let our inner child come out to play. And to remember that ultimately, this is the season of wonder. And what's more wondrous than a hushed blanket of white as far as the eye can see, broken only by the familiar call of loved ones and the twinkling lights of home?

Among the gray skies and bare trees of midwinter, a fresh snowfall can change everything. It can smooth corners, soften edges, and give us a crisp white page upon which we can write our next adventure and, together, our happiest memories.

Snowflake Science

Under the microscope, I found that snowflakes were miracles of beauty . . . every crystal was a masterpiece of design, and no one design was ever repeated.

—Wilson "Snowflake" Bentley

Surely you've heard that "no two snowflakes are alike." The man to prove this theory was Wilson A. Bentley, from the snowy town of Jericho, Vermont. In 1885, he became the first person to photograph a single snow crystal— and went on to capture 5,000 more. You can see some of these amazing images for yourself in his books *Snow Crystals* and *Snowflakes in Photographs.* You can also read about the man himself in the award-winning children's book *Snowflake Bentley,* by Jaqueline Briggs Martin.

According to the National Center for Atmospheric Research in Boulder, CO, the average snowflake falls at a speed of approximately three feet per second. When you're out in a snowstorm, that may seem pretty fast, but it's really only about two miles per hour.

Snow People

Skiers and snowboarders love dry, powdery snow. But those of us who like to get out there and play wish for the kind of snow that's wet and sticky. Terrible for driving, but terrific for stockpiling snowballs, building forts, and crafting snow creatures of all kinds.

If America has a "snowman expert," it may just be a man named Jim Sysko. In 1999, he and 60 volunteers built Angus, World's Largest Snowman in Bethel, Maine. At 113 feet and 7 inches tall, he towered 17 feet over the previous record holder in Japan. And he was estimated to weigh in at 9 million pounds.

Here are a few tips from Jim and his wife:

❄ Build your snowman in a shady spot.

❄ If the snow is powdery, sprinkle it with water from the hose or a watering can.

❄ Flatten the balls of snow before adding another.

❄ Get help with the middle section—it can be heavy.

❄ Pack reinforcing snow around the base, waist, and neck to keep your snowman stable.

❄ Get creative with materials. (Chow mein noodles make a wild hairdo!)

THE ABOMINABLE SNOWMAN

Also known as the Yeti (the Tibetan word for "magical creature") the abominable snowman is described as being six- to eight-feet tall and covered in hair. He's thought to live high in the Himalayan mountains.

Though many explorers claim to have come upon the creature or his footprints, others say he's simply a large bear, ape, or just a figment of their imagination. Nevertheless, the abominable snowman has appeared in literature, TV, and movies and is almost never as abominable as he may seem.

MR. SANDMAN

You're not likely to find much snow in sunny California. But that's no reason to forgo favorite winter activities. In cities like San Diego and Los Angeles, sand stands in for snow at the Holiday Sandman Competition. A corporate sponsor provides tools and some sand-sculpting training, while local families provide the imagination. The best sandman (that jolly, happy soul!) earns his creators a $1,000 gift certificate to a national department store and the honor of having made the "hottest" snowman.

Sledding

*I*f you grew up in a place where winters were snowy, you may remember the exact sled you dragged to the local hill. Whether you said goodbye to it a long time ago or have it buried somewhere in the garage, it may not take much to get you excited about sledding.

The first major manufacturer of sleds was the Paris Manufacturing Corporation of South Paris, Maine. The sleds were hand-painted by Henry Morton and his wife. In the 1870s, mass-produced versions were available from the Montgomery Ward catalog, priced anywhere from $.60 to $1.15.

The most famous American sled just may be the Flexible Flyer, made by Pennsylvania farmer Samuel Leeds Allen. The sled had a pair of steel blades and—a major improvement—handlebars for steering! By 1915, the Flexible Flyer company was selling 2,000 sleds a day.

After World War II, every baby boomer had a sled on his or her Christmas list. There was more variety then; for instance, the "saucer sled" was a huge hit. So was the "Batwing" sled (fashioned after the hit TV show).

Today, you're likely to see all kinds of sleds on the hill: metal saucers, inflatable donuts, plastic toboggans, and even a few Flexible Flyers, since you can buy a replica version at a specialty toy or gadget store.

SIGNIFICANT SLEDS

* There's an original Flexible Flyer on display in the Smithsonian Institute in Washington, D.C.

* The famous Rosebud sled from Citizen Kane was sold at auction in 1982 for $60,500. The buyer was Steven Spielberg.

* The toboggan—from the Algonquian word *odabaggan*—is a Native-American invention. They were used to carry game or supplies over the snow. Often, they were pulled by women.

Skating

The earliest ice-skaters probably skated for transportation—on skates made with sharpened animal bones attached to the feet with leather straps. Dutch skaters were the first to use iron blades—and were the ones to invent the kind of double-edged blade that allows skaters to move without poles. Called the "Dutch Roll," the move is still used by skaters today.

By the 1700s, ice-skating was a popular winter pastime in Europe, and it quickly spread to North America. Figure skating for men, women, and pairs became Olympic sports in 1908.

The largest natural rink is the Rideau Canal Skateway in Ottawa, Canada. The canal is 4.8 miles long. That's the size of 90 Olympic-sized skating rinks.

Wollman Skating Rink in New York City's Central Park was built in 1949. On its opening day, 300,000 skaters glided across the ice. Today, it sees about 4,000 skaters a day and offers all sorts of skating fun, including skating school, ice hockey, and birthday parties. Each lap around the rink comes with a magical view of Manhattan and, if it's a clear night, a sky full of stars.

When the temperature drops in Amsterdam, the canals become sparkling highways through the city. Residents and visitors alike strap on their skates and glide away to the sound of classical music and stop every so often to buy a heartwarming beverage from a little stall set up right on the ice.

If you live in a place where the sun simply won't stop shining, try one of the local indoor rinks. At DisneyICE in Anaheim, California, there are two rinks (NHL and Olympic-sized), so skaters have all the room they need to practice figure eights, triple toe loops, slap shots—or just skating in a straight line without falling down.

Not a Snowplow Was Stirring

*M*ore likely to spend Christmas with sunscreen than snowdrifts? You're not alone. The National Climatic Data Center estimates that, on average, one-third of the U.S. population lives in areas with virtually no chance of a Yuletide snowfall. Not to mention the entire Southern Hemisphere, for whom December 25 occurs during summer! Here's a look at how those living in sunny places around the world celebrate Christmas—without snow.

EVERGREEN OPTIONAL

No spruce tree to spruce up? No problem! In the West African nation of Liberia, families adorn palm trees with bells. Those celebrating Christmas in India decorate mango trees. And in Bangladesh, paths to churches and homes are lined with pairs of arched banana trees, lit by oil lamps.

A NOT-SO-SILENT NIGHT

In South American countries such as Brazil, Christmas is cause for an all-out festival. Without the need for a single snowplow, celebrations are taken into the streets— complete with firecrackers, brass bands, and dancing.

CHRISTMAS ISLAND

This is perhaps the only place where it's truly Christmas year-round—but it stays 100% snow-free. This small tropical island, located northwest of Australia in the Indian Ocean, got its name when a British captain discovered it on Christmas Day, 1643.

WHITE CHRISTMAS GUARANTEED

Unless you live in Alaska, the mountains, or far northern states, you may spend most Decembers merely dreaming of a white Christmas. Based on averages over the past 30 years, The National Climatic Data Center lists only five continental U.S. cities that stand a 100% chance of at least one inch of snow on Christmas Day.

> Marquette, MI
> Sault Ste Marie, MI
> Hibbing, MN
> International Falls, MN
> Stampede Pass, WA

WHAT ARE THE ODDS?

So what's that chance that your Christmas will be white? There's no guarantee (and granted, Christmas is the season of miracles . . .), but before you place your bets, you might want to check the National Climatic Data Center's map of Christmas snow likelihood. (Where do you fall on snowfall? See for yourself at srh.noaa.gov/oun/climate/christmas/.)

Stars!

The weather's always colder in winter, but the season is filled with the brightest stars and some of the most amazing astronomical events. Many of them are all but invisible to the naked eye. But some are so fantastic, you'll be willing to brave the weather for a heavenly glimpse.

Check out what's happening up there at **skytonight.com/observing**.

Frankly, I don't know how they do it. You know, the folks who make those amazing snow people and end up with their pictures in the paper? For us, it's too darn cold to spend so much time outside in the winter. My son, Patrick, came up with a solution years ago. After a good snowfall, we fill a couple of small garbage bags and throw them in the freezer. Then, when the dog days of summer roll around, one of us will remember the stash, haul it out to the front lawn, and we'll make a snowman—complete with sunglasses, a baseball cap, and a plastic lei. Watching folks drive by and taking long, bemused looks at our yard is a great reward—plus knowing that, at least on that one day, we have the best snowman in town!

—Lisa Jacobson, Clear Lake, IA

Real Traditions

When we moved from downtown Albany to a farm, we wanted a way to celebrate New Year's and enjoy our friends and families. We decided on a slumber party. We prepared a feast, lit a bonfire, set off fireworks at midnight, and everyone sledded and skated until they were completely exhausted and collapsed wherever there was bed space or sleeping bag space or any space at all! It was such a hit that we've been doing it for 13 years. I've watched my children and my friends' children turn from wobbly toddlers to speed demons and hockey pros—with a few figure skaters thrown in. Now the kids are a bit older, but New Year's still has a special sweetness—that neither weather nor distance nor teenage disdain for being home on New Year's will keep us from continuing.

—Meave Tooher, Coxsackie, NY

One year, my fiancé and I both found ourselves laid off during the holidays. Not ideal, but we decided to make the best we could out of the situation. We were hard at work every morning looking for jobs, but we made a daily tradition of having lunch together (something we could never do before!), then walking over to the town skating rink. Since it was the middle of the day, we had the whole place to ourselves! And it didn't cost a thing! We'd skate around for about an hour or so, then we'd change back into our shoes and head home for tea or hot chocolate. Fortunately, we're both back at work. But unfortunately, there's a lot less time for playing around. So we make it a point to go at least once a month in the winter season.

—Sarah Cole, Stowe, VT

Has this book inspired any cheerful
Christmas traditions or family festivities?
If you're a kid from 1 to 92, we'd love to
hear what fun you've had in these pages.

Please drop us a line by mail:

Hallmark Cards, Inc.
Book Feedback
Mail Drop 215
2501 McGee Street
Kansas City, MO 64108

or e-mail:

booknotes@hallmark.com